Colin Painter

At Home with Art

AF378453

National Touring Exhibitions

sbc

Published on the occasion of *At Home with Art*, an exhibition organised jointly by the Tate Gallery, London and National Touring Exhibitions from the Hayward Gallery, London, on behalf of the Arts Council of England.

Exhibition launched at the Tate Gallery, London,
15 November 1999 – 13 February 2000
before touring throughout the UK

Exhibition curated by Colin Painter
Exhibition organised by Miranda Stacey, Hayward Gallery,
and Ben Tufnell, Tate Gallery

Catalogue designed by Peter Campbell
Printed in England by P.J. Print

Published by Hayward Gallery Publishing, London SE1 8XX
© The South Bank Centre 1999
Text © Colin Painter 1999
Artworks © The Artists

Photographic Credits
Front cover: top centre © Anne Painter, all other photographs © David Morgan
Back cover: © Anne Painter
All photographs © Anne Painter apart from those on the following pages:
© Ant Critchfield, 1999, p. 47; Prudence Cuming, London, pp. 35 (top) & 59;
Carsten Eisfeld, Berlin, p. 11; Antony Gormley, p. 29 (top); Hajime Inoue, p. 41; Gerry Johansson, p. 35 (bottom); © Helmut Kunde, Kiel, 1999, p. 29 (bottom); Randall Michelson, Los Angeles, p. 17 (bottom); David Morgan, London, pp. 15, 27, 28, 33, 39, 45, 47 (bottom right), 51, 56 (top right), 57, 58, 62; Helge Mundt, p. 23 (top); Gareth Winters, p. 23 (bottom).

ISBN 1 85332 200 8

This catalogue is not intended to be used for authentication or related purposes. The South Bank Board accepts no liability for any errors or omissions which the catalogue may inadvertently contain.

This publication is distributed in North and South America and Canada by the University of California Press, 2120 Berkeley Way, Berkeley, California 94720, and elsewhere by Cornerhouse Publications.

Hayward Gallery Publishing titles are distributed outside North and South America and Canada by Cornerhouse Publications, 70 Oxford Street, Manchester M1 5NH (tel: 0161 200 1503; fax: 0161 237 1504; email: publications@cornerhouse.org).

Front cover: the artists' works. Back cover: the artists with the householders.
Top (left to right): Angela Bulloch, Tony Cragg, Richard Deacon.
Middle (left to right): Antony Gormley, Anish Kapoor, Permindar Kaur.
Bottom (left to right): David Mach, Richard Wentworth, Alison Wilding.

Contemporary art is rarely considered or encountered in the context of everyday life in the home, being mainly seen in museums, galleries and public spaces. Yet it is in homes that people express their personal taste and make commitments to images and objects of all kinds.

To challenge the stereotypical view of contemporary art as somehow alien to the values of ordinary domestic life, Professor Colin Painter conceived the idea of commissioning artists to design a work of art for the home which would be made available to a mass market. After three years of planning and negotiation, a unique collaboration involving the Tate Gallery, Homebase, National Touring Exhibitions from the Hayward Gallery, the Arts Council of England's 'New Audiences Programme' and Wimbledon School of Art has come to fruition. Nine of Britain's leading sculptors have created works for mass production and sale at modest prices in Homebase stores.

This publication accompanies an exhibition of drawings, prototypes, photographs and the final objects themselves, organized jointly by the Tate Gallery and National Touring Exhibitions. It opened at the Tate Gallery and is touring in an expanded form to galleries and arts centres throughout Britain. The exhibition and publication document the project through its various stages.

Every step in the process has been co-ordinated and overseen by Colin Painter, and our thanks are due firstly to him, for his vision, determination and whole-hearted commitment. The artists' unanimously favourable response to his proposal surely owed as much to his infectious enthusiasm and evident integrity as to the originality and promise of his idea. We thank them for entering so generously into the spirit of a complex and multi-faceted undertaking. The families with whom they were paired responded with interest and good humour, and their contributions are recorded in the following pages, accompanied by Anne Painter's illuminating photographs. My thanks go also to Roger Malbert, the Hayward's Senior Curator, National Touring Exhibitions, who first championed Colin Painter's proposal here, and to Sandy Nairne and Andrew Brighton who did so at the Tate, to Miranda Stacey, who has organized the exhibition on behalf of the Hayward Gallery in close collaboration with the Tate Gallery, and to Peter Campbell, who has designed the catalogue with characteristic skill and enthusiasm.

Homebase has shown exceptional boldness and imagination in taking on this unprecedented experiment, providing the funding which made mass production possible. The project was also supported by Wimbledon School of Art, which funded the research towards the production of prototypes, and by the Arts Council of England's 'New Audiences Programme' which supported many aspects of the project, in particular documentary displays in Homebase stores. It also funded the management, monitoring and evaluation of the project and research into peoples' attitudes to contemporary art in a new context. Latchmere Junior School, Kingston upon Thames, provided the focus for the recruitment of the nine participating households, to whom we also extend our thanks.

Susan Ferleger Brades
Director, Hayward Gallery

Acknowledgements

Many people and organizations have made enormous contributions to the realization of this project. I am pleased to have the opportunity to thank them here. I am particularly grateful to the households and the artists for the generosity with which they participated.

Thanks also to Lord Sainsbury of Preston Candover KG, Nicholas Serota and Sandy Nairne, for early help in launching the project.

To list all the individuals working for the organizations cited below would be impossible, but there are a few names that must be mentioned because of the scale of their contributions: in particular Rosey Blackmore of Tate Gallery Publishing and Paul Housego of Homebase. I would also like to thank Peter Allen, Kate Bell, David Black, Andrew Brighton, Hannah Broke-Smith, Nigel Bullivant, Peter Campbell, Tom Caveney, Eileen Daly, Stephen Deuchar, Judy Dobias, Rosalind Freeborn, William Furlong, Mary Van Hogermeer, Carl Jones, Phillip Lazell, Claire Longfield, Roger Malbert, Paul Moore, Rob Robinson, Bob Russell, Miranda Stacey, Kim Tran, Ben Tufnell, Sally Warren and David Washington.

I would also like to thank the manufacturers who mass produced the products: José Machado de Almeida, Portugal; Granton Ragg Ltd., Sheffield; G.H. Plumber & Co. Ltd., West Molsey; The Royal Doulton Company, Stoke-on-Trent; Stafford Rubber Company Ltd., Cannock; Spear and Jackson plc., Wednesbury, with technical support from Delcam UK and Welwyn Lighting Co., Welwyn Garden City.

Last but certainly not least, thanks to Anne Painter, whose involvement and support have extended far beyond the role of photographer. Indispensable …

Colin Painter

This is the story of a project. It is important to emphasize that the story is told from a personal perspective. In particular, I take responsibility for the statement of the project's purposes. The nine artists did not participate in the project on the basis that they necessarily share, in every detail, my reasons for organizing it. I hope some sense of their various views comes through in their statements here.

The project is an experiment in connecting the work of artists from the contemporary art world with a wider public through mass-producing works for the home and making them available for sale in the mass market. [1]

It was Richard Deacon who suggested to me that the project itself might be seen as a prototype.

Why Homes?

For many people their homes provide the most meaningful and intense relationship with aesthetic and symbolic objects.

Though the majority of people in Britain may not be interested in contemporary art, we all surround ourselves in our homes with images and aesthetic objects which are acquired in a wide variety of ways. What's more, though we may not think about it very often, these objects are of great importance to us. As well as having aesthetic significance, they represent commitments, events, anniversaries, people, rites of passage. When we talk about these objects we find ourselves talking about our lives, our beliefs, our relationships, our mortality.

We give objects many meanings not intended by their makers. In fact, the things we own have an amalgamation of meanings. The aesthetic object can also be a religious object, a souvenir, a reminder of a friend, a piece of furniture, a part of the decor – perhaps a work of art. Distinctions between the functional and non-functional are often blurred. It is in this combination of roles and meanings that art can become part of life.

While the impulse to have objects and images around us may be common, the words of householders in these pages show that there are differences from home to home in the nature and mix of things, the ways they are understood, the meanings they hold. The images and objects in the homes in which we grow up are presented to us as 'normality' and, implicitly, as models of their kind. They inform our sense of who we are, our place in the world, our tastes. They offer examples of what is right, true and good. We do not experience this as 'learning' or 'education'. It is a matter of contagion, permeation and socialization. When we make our own homes, we continue the process of identifying and understanding ourselves, refining our tastes, through the things around us. We connect our lives with others by giving and receiving objects for the home. It is difficult to imagine a more important or influential place for the work of artists. Arguably, it is more formative and important than the art gallery, the museum or the education system.

Yet, for most people, work by artists from the professional world inhabited by the nine artists participating in this project is absent. Since the project addresses this absence it is necessary to consider the causes of it and, at the same time, attempt the difficult task of offering some definition of the 'contemporary art world' which the project sets out to connect more widely with the home.

Contemporary Art

There is a lot of image and object making going on today. Since it is in the present, it is all 'contemporary'. Some of it is called 'art'; some is not. You can buy images and objects from all sorts of places – galleries, mail-order catalogues, gift shops, furniture shops, market stalls, garden centres. When I started this project Homebase was selling a garden sculpture of a lion. Only a small minority of these places sell the work of contemporary artists of the kind involved in this project.

Forced to point to the kind of art I mean by 'contemporary art', for the purposes of this project I might say that it is, broadly, the kind of art in the modern collection at the Tate Gallery, the kind of art taught in the Fine Art Departments of our art schools, the kind of art associated with the Turner Prize. But it would be misleading to identify 'contemporary art' with any particular kind of works. Rather, I mean a professional culture of image and object making – impossible to delineate with precision, full of diversity and contradictions, but nonetheless real.

It is a professional culture that is self-conscious, aware of its past, experimental, critically rigorous and concerned about the effects of its products. It is the site of an informed debate about what images and objects can mean and achieve. It is a world preoccupied with the knowledge that images and objects have effect, that they influence our perceptions, that we define ourselves through the images and descriptions we adopt of the world, shape ourselves through the shapes we make and use. Perhaps most importantly, I believe that it is a world in which that knowledge is most clearly held with moral responsibility. It is this responsible commitment, knowledge, range of skills and abilities – rather than any particular catalogue of works – that should be more widely available to people in their homes, there to participate in, and contribute to, life. This project is a modest experiment towards that end.

This description of contemporary art is in stark contrast to that perpetuated by media hype, flip commentary and strident curatorship which has characterized it in the public mind as sensationalist, irresponsible and sometimes just plain silly. It is a characterization that may, at times, be justified but the work of the nine sculptors who have participated in this project clearly defies it as a generalization. Sadly, their work, and that of others like them, is unfamiliar to the majority of people in Britain and makes limited contact with their lives.

A major reason for this is that the contemporary art world has tended to marginalize the home as a serious location for art. It has been viewed as trivial – not as a subject for art but as a location for it. This is not to say that there is any objection, in principle, to contemporary art ending up in homes so long as that possibility does not affect its conception, critical reception, exhibition or distribution.[2] The roles that art might play in the home are considered irrelevant or trifling as criteria for judging work. To say 'I wouldn't hang that on my living-room wall' is thought to exemplify philistinism, a lack of regard for the intrinsic characteristics of the work as 'art'.

'Ultimately, in the eyes of the avant-garde, being undomestic came to serve as a guarantee of being art.'
Reed, C. (ed), *Not at Home*, Thames and Hudson, London, 1996, p. 7

This is closely connected with a powerful rhetoric – principally from commentators and critics rather than artists – to the effect that contemporary art is to be defined in terms of 'challenge' or 'disturbance'. Contemporary art might often challenge but it is misleading as its defining emphasis. Not only is much of it celebratory and positive, but that which 'challenges' might be more appropriately and constructively described as inviting new perceptions, raising questions, offering new possibilities. The denial of the celebratory and confirmatory functions of art inevitably leads to the marginalization of the home as a location.

The contemporary art world's rejection of the domestic, coupled with the separation between notions of fine art and 'applied' art, amounts to a rejection of most of the uses that people have for images and objects. Some of these uses may seem irrelevant to prevailing notions of 'art' but they are ways into lives and, as such, offer the opportunity for interaction with art. The fact that a sculpture might be bought to be part of the decor, a souvenir or a gift, does not eliminate its potential to have effect as sculpture. In fact, it provides the opportunity for it to have effect.

The marginalization of the domestic also means that contemporary artists of the kind participating in this project rarely make work with the home in mind, nor is their work made available for purchase where things for the home are sold to a wide public. This, in turn, means that contemporary art is unfamiliar to most people. Not encountering it as part of their normal lives, they do not feel 'at home' with it.

And it is familiarity and contagion, as distinct from 'education' and 'knowledge', that should be the emphasis. Contemporary art should find its way into people's lives in the same way as gardening or football. Both require knowledge but it begins at home – with family and friends – not seeming like 'knowledge' at all.

At this point I should emphasize that I am not suggesting that all contemporary art should be domestic in conception, scale or aspiration – merely that the home is an important and undervalued location. Participation in that environment could engender a broader public interest in contemporary art.

The Project

There are three main obstacles to contemporary art finding a place in more peoples' homes. The first has already been discussed – the attitude to the domestic in the contemporary art world. Second, most places where contemporary art is made available for sale are unfamilar and forbidding territory for many people – indeed in some cases you have to ring a bell to gain entry. Interestingly, artists have tried to escape the confines of 'white box' galleries by making work for all sorts of locations – factories, hospitals, schools and public outdoor sites – but rarely the home.[3] Third, contemporary art is generally sold at higher prices than most people can afford.

Through the collaboration of an unusual range of agencies and individuals, this project, which has taken nearly four years to realize, addresses all three of these obstacles. In addition, it brings the underlying issues into debate through the associated exhibition, initially at the Tate Gallery, London, and then being toured for two years by National Touring Exhibitions from the Hayward Gallery.

Each of the nine sculptors was asked to take part in a project which was an experiment in participation in domestic life, as distinct from an invitation to comment upon it. It was a requirement that they should each begin by visiting a household to observe the way in which objects and images were displayed and understood there. This was to ensure a genuine focus on domestic realities. We all think we know what homes are like – we live in one, grew up in one – but it is illuminating to enter a strange home with the specific purpose of observing what appears to be happening there, to talk with the householders about the things around them, how they come to be there, what they're doing. Perhaps it was 'consciousness raising'. Antony Gormley described it as 'grounding the project', a formulation that I happily adopted.

The purpose was to make a mass-produced object for sale to the general public, so it was obviously not the intention that the householders should be treated as clients or that the work should be site specific. The households were 'launching pads'. The relationship with the householders was reciprocal. Where possible, they visited the artists' studios or attended exhibitions that were open during the period. As the artists' statements show, the households had varying degrees of influence on the subsequent work. It is also clear from the words of the householders that the homes shared similarities as well as many differences. Households were recruited with the help of the head-teacher of Latchmere Junior School, Kingston upon Thames, who invited volunteers from parents and staff – both teaching and non-teaching. There is no suggestion that they are 'representative' in any way, they merely offer a variety of contexts.

It is important to stress that the artists were not asked to operate as 'designers'. They were simply asked to bring their preoccupations, knowledge, sensibilities and skills to the domestic arena. It was left to them to decide whether to make a functional or non-functional object. One of the fascinating aspects of the project has been to see which way each artist went. It has also drawn attention to difficulties in decisively distinguishing between the functional and non-functional. Familiar debates about the relative status of fine art and functional objects emerge. Is Alison Wilding's ceramic sculpture lessened because it might be used as a bowl? Is Permindar Kaur's imagery less worthy of attention because it appears on a shower curtain?

Following the contact with the households, it was for the artists to give some indication of what they might want to make. This was no simple matter since much depended on what was possible, the availability, limitations and characteristics of particular materials, the realities of mass-production processes, the financial parameters – the project required that the mass-produced object retailed at under £90 (in the event, significantly lower prices were achieved). With the help of Homebase I arranged the connections and negotiations between artists and manufacturers. The process began and developed differently in each case, as the accounts in the following pages show. Incidentally, Homebase did not interfere in the process after helping to identify manufacturers. There was not a hint of censorship. One of Tony Cragg's proposals – the baby's bottle – did not proceed but this was simply because Homebase does not stock baby products.

The discussions between artists and manufacturers were intriguing, each having to re-think in the light of the other's imperatives. All of this took place within a fierce schedule. The artists visited their households between December '98 and February '99. The objects were to be ready for mass production to begin by June '99 with the products being available for sale in October. In fact, there was some slippage in the schedule.

Each artist carefully supervised the evolution of the work from initial idea to mass production. The products are not mass-produced objects with the work of artists added to them. They are not reproductions – copies of originals that retain higher authenticity. They are an unlimited edition of objects, conceived and realized within the materials and processes of mass production. In the art world the term 'multiple' is applicable but the project puts pressure on this concept. It is difficult to see how the term 'multiple' distinguishes these objects from other mass-produced objects of their genre – functional or non-functional. The difficulty of distinguishing the functional from the non-functional has already been mentioned.

Whatever the philosophical difficulties of categorization, it is the case that in different homes different values are attached to the original, the limited edition, the multiple, the reproduction. Through the involvement of Homebase it has been possible to make the works available for sale where a wide public goes to buy things for the home. People will measure them in relation to their own priorities and values. They will be able to encounter them, perhaps by accident, within the array of other things that they are considering buying for their homes, or for the homes of others. They will have the opportunity to see in them the potential to fulfil roles in their lives – roles perhaps unforeseen by the artists.

At time of writing the public response is unknown.

Colin Painter

Notes

1. I have elaborated on the ideas which led to this project at length elsewhere. See *At Home with Constable's Cornfield*, National Gallery Publications, 1996, and, particularly, *The Uses of an Artist: Constable in Constable Country Now*, Ipswich Borough Council Museums, 1998 (distributed by Tate Gallery Publishing).

2. In the context of commissions attitudes are more positive. There the location of the work (including the home) is more likely to be accepted as an influence. Reservations about the domestic are also less evident within the grander notion of 'architecture'. It is the 'ordinary home' (not usually graced with the status of 'architecture') perhaps typified by notions of suburbia, which presents the biggest problem. Commissions here are rare.

3. The home has been used as a gallery, as a space for installations and, of course, as the 'subject' for work. The reference here is to work being conceived and made available to take its place within domestic life.

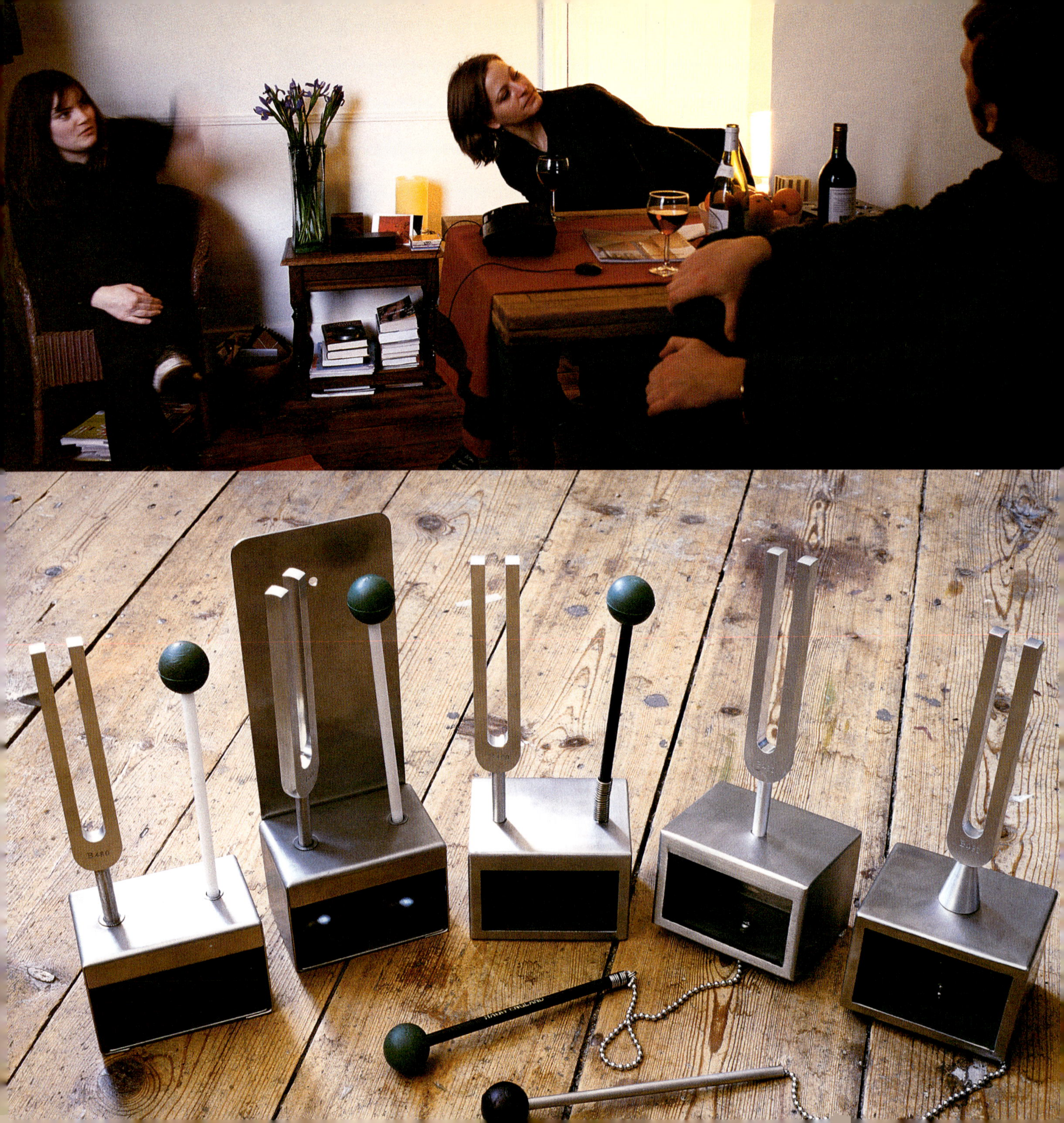

Angela Bulloch

Colin Painter: The possibility of making something involving a tuning fork arose for Angela Bulloch in her initial conversation with Vanessa and Kevin when visiting their home. She was the only artist to be that close to elements of the eventual outcome so early. She shared a catholic interest in music with them both.

The possibility of wall-mounting a tuning fork led to discussions with Bob Russell, Engineering Manager of Granton Ragg Ltd., tuning fork manufacturers in Sheffield. Russell produced a sequence of prototypes from Bulloch's preliminary drawings, offering each for her attention and modification.

From an early stage there were two main approaches in Bulloch's mind. One was the possibility of mounting the hammer on a spring beside the fork so that it could be levered back and released. The other, which was ultimately adopted, had the hammer hanging loose. Bulloch's proposals extended the normal parameters of tuning fork manufacture considerably. 'We really had to stretch the imagination in applying solutions to overcome manufacturing and assembly difficulties, whilst satisfying Angela Bulloch's requirements,' said Russell.

Technical problems in mounting the fork, maintaining its resonance when fixed to a wall and eliminating unwanted vibration had to be solved in harmony with the artist's visual priorities. This process was not without its tensions as Russell encountered and solved new practical difficulties at each stage and took the initiative in building the solutions into the next prototype, changing its appearance in ways that were not anticipated by Bulloch. However, the interaction proved a strength and the piece is a fascinating product of the meeting of engineering and artistic priorities.

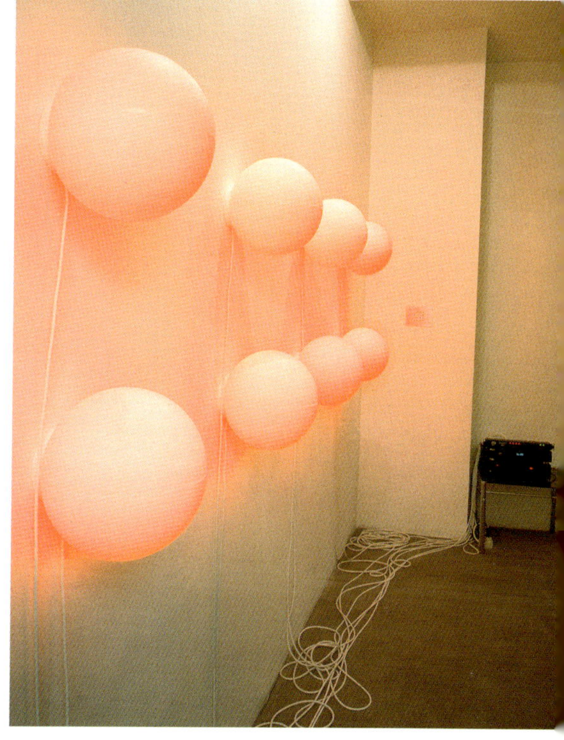

VISUAL MUSIC 8, 1998
8 POLYCARBONATE SPHERES, RED LIGHT BULBS, LIGHT
CONTROLLER, CD PLAYER, AMPLIFIER, 17 CDS
PRIVATE COLLECTION, TURIN

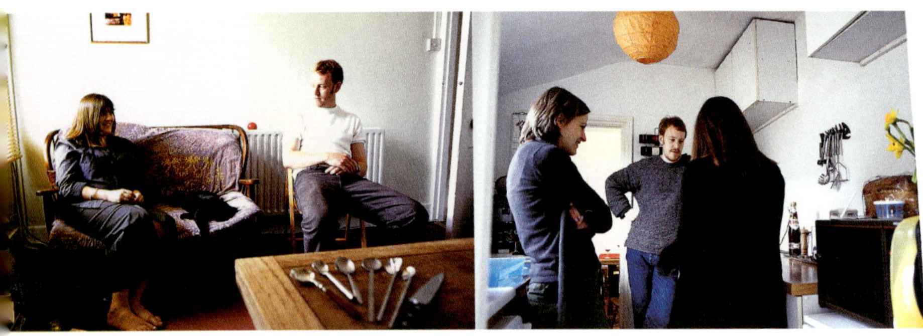

1   2

Kevin Hogston and **Vanessa Howe**

VANESSA: Colour is important to me. Most things we buy are either red or green for some reason.

KEVIN: The colours of walls affect everything. We spent a lot of time choosing colours for the rooms and we've ended up echoing the colours we had in our old flat – which we hadn't chosen . . . We usually disagree about where things should be placed. Vanessa has very strong convictions about how things should be arranged.

VANESSA: Kevin doesn't take much interest – until things are actually here. I buy most of them.

KEVIN: Unless it's something I particularly dislike I go along with Vanessa's judgement. We're making a home together. It's a compromise . . . When I just had a bedroom at home everything was to do with me. It was my statement. It was a Tottenham Hotspur environment. Now it's a shared environment. I'd like people who come in to think, 'That's different. That's tasteful'.

VANESSA: I would like to gut the whole house and start from scratch. None of our furniture is stuff I'd buy from choice. I'm always imagining what I would have if I could do exactly what I wanted. We went to Cornwall at Easter and saw lots of things there that I wanted to get. There was a sculpture in particular – but it was about £600. If I could afford things like that I'd love to have them.

VANESSA: There's a dining-room shop that I love. It's got all this Victorian cutlery, special sugar spoons and things – things you don't really need but they're so lovely. I like to use old cutlery or modern things like a spoon that's a drinking straw as well. Things that are functional and decorative appeal to me.

KEVIN: One of my prize possessions is a very cheap looking kitchen knife. I was given it by my Home Economics teacher when I left the sixth form. I was the only boy that did Home Economics A level. Now I do all the cooking so I spend a lot of time in the kitchen. The things in there are more important to me than anywhere else. It's a bit of a clutter, but that's the way we are.

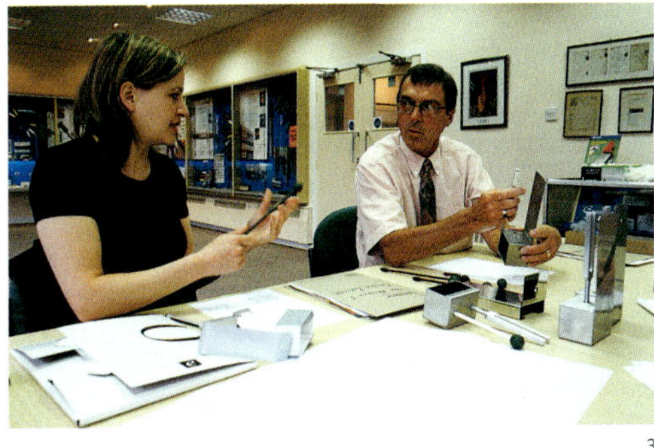

Angela Bulloch

Art always exists in some kind of context and this project creates a very particular set of contexts –
Homebase and the Tate, for example. Having a particular home as another context was a very useful
focus since the object would ultimately end up in such a place, someone's house that is.

> Kevin had a very special knife that had been presented to him by his domestic science teacher
> and Vanessa had a collection of spoons. So I thought of making a fork which would go to make
> up the traditional three. I did think about making a knife, fork and spoon set but I wanted to
> make a more symbolic object rather than something purely functional. That led me to thinking
> of a fork which crossed a few boundaries in other ways – like the fact that they both liked
> music and they had things around them they had given value to. I wanted to make a fork which
> might have some symbolic as well as functional value.

I liked the idea of having something mass produced and potentially becoming a popular item –
reaching a lot of people. I also liked the idea of having something both on sale in Homebase and on
show at the Tate. I like that connection.

> I was interested in making an object which reflects the idea of consensual harmony. A note is
> an abstract measure of sound which civilization has agreed upon. Every time a 'B' is struck, it is
> a reminder of that order, which I find beautiful. I like the idea of making something that's the
> same in every piece. The sound is exactly the same in every tuning fork tuned to 'B' and that's
> the mass-produced idea.

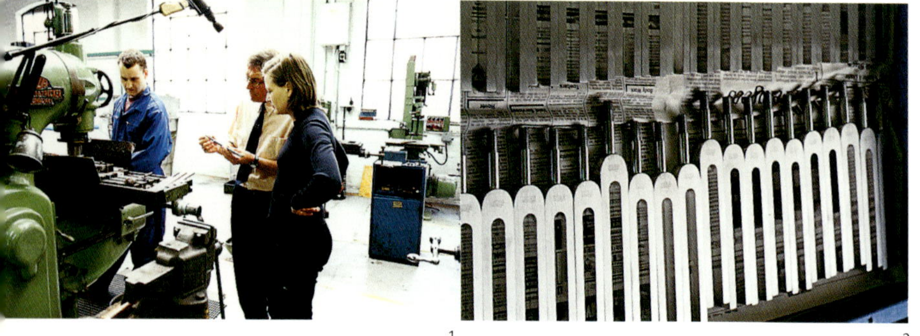

1 ANGELA BULLOCH IN THE MACHINE ROOM, GRANTON RAGG LTD.

2 TUNING FORKS READY FOR ASSEMBLY, GRANTON RAGG LTD.

3 ANGELA BULLOCH'S SKETCH FOR AN EARLY PROTOTYPE

The way we have all collectively agreed, somehow, that certain frequencies of sound are given significance within a scale – it's a bit like conforming to standard measurements – how did we actually arrive there? We have to have markers. The note 'B' is one of those markers. It symbolizes the human will to organize the world – to measure things. That kind of will within society is a beautiful thing.

Striking the same note is quite a civilizing idea. When a choir sings exactly the same note in unison there's something marvellous about it. It's like producing a very pared down musical instrument – only capable of making one note.

I chose 'B' for a few reasons. There's the play with words or letters – a 'B' is just simply a 'B' in many languages. The piece is titled *A'B'*. Then my initials are AB. There is a play on the singularity of it – *A'B'* – yet there are lots of them. It's an economic way of saying quite a few things in two letters.

There's a whole science of using notes to affect the body through vibrations. The note 'B' is the one associated with the chakra at the crown of the head. I chose 'B' because I play in a band and that note is one I play a lot. I've listened to and played that note an awful lot lately.

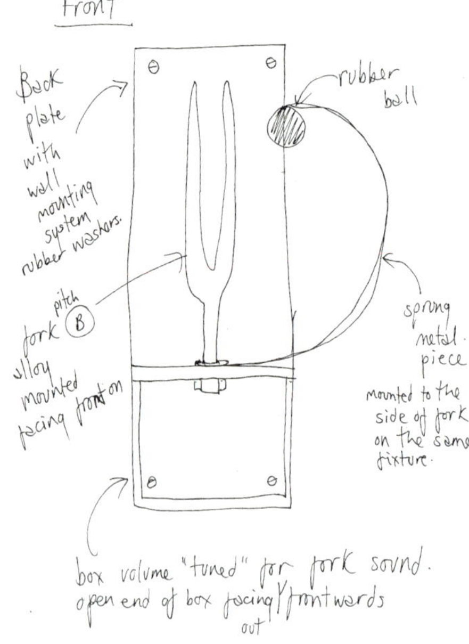

3

THE FINAL TUNING FORK

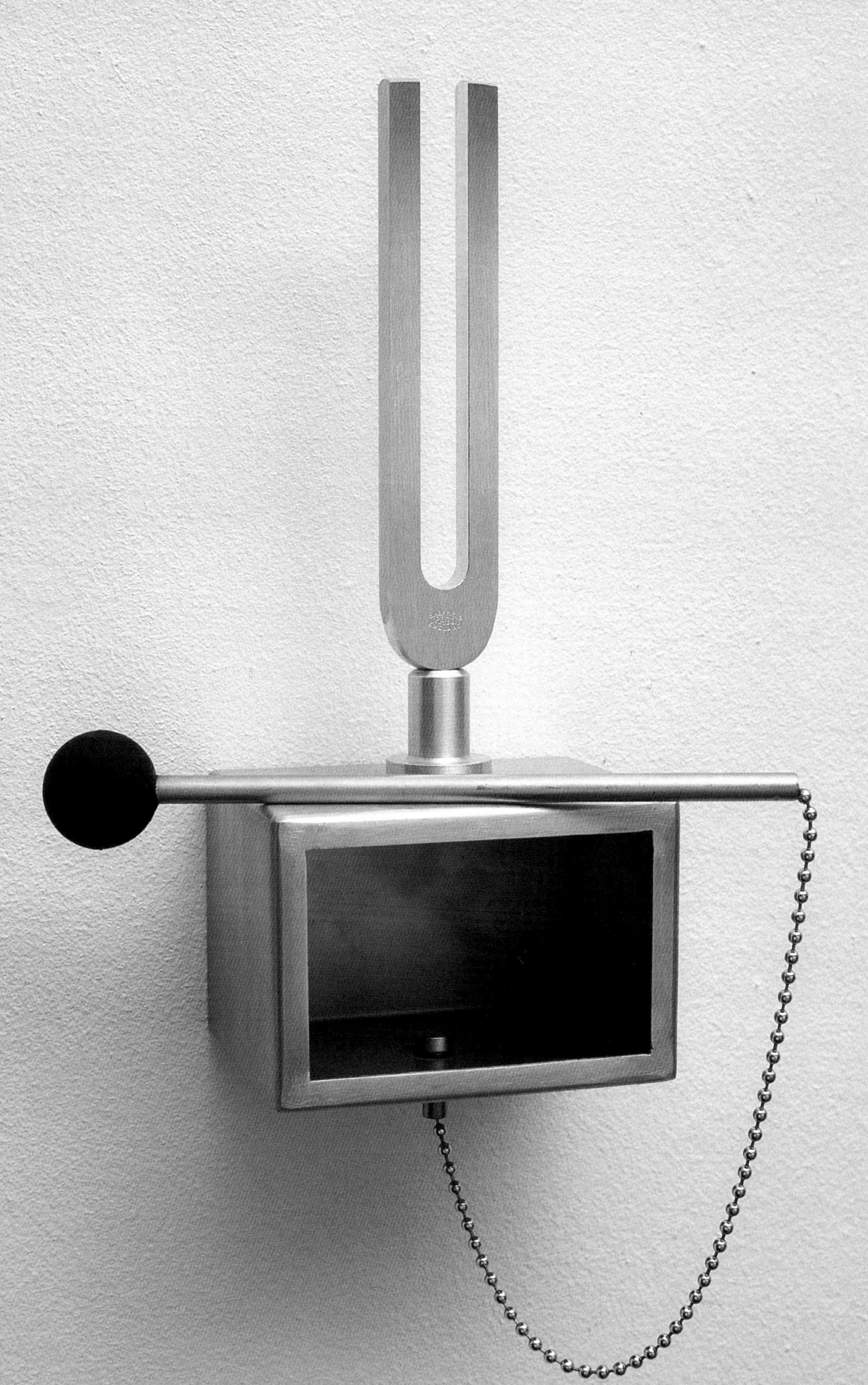

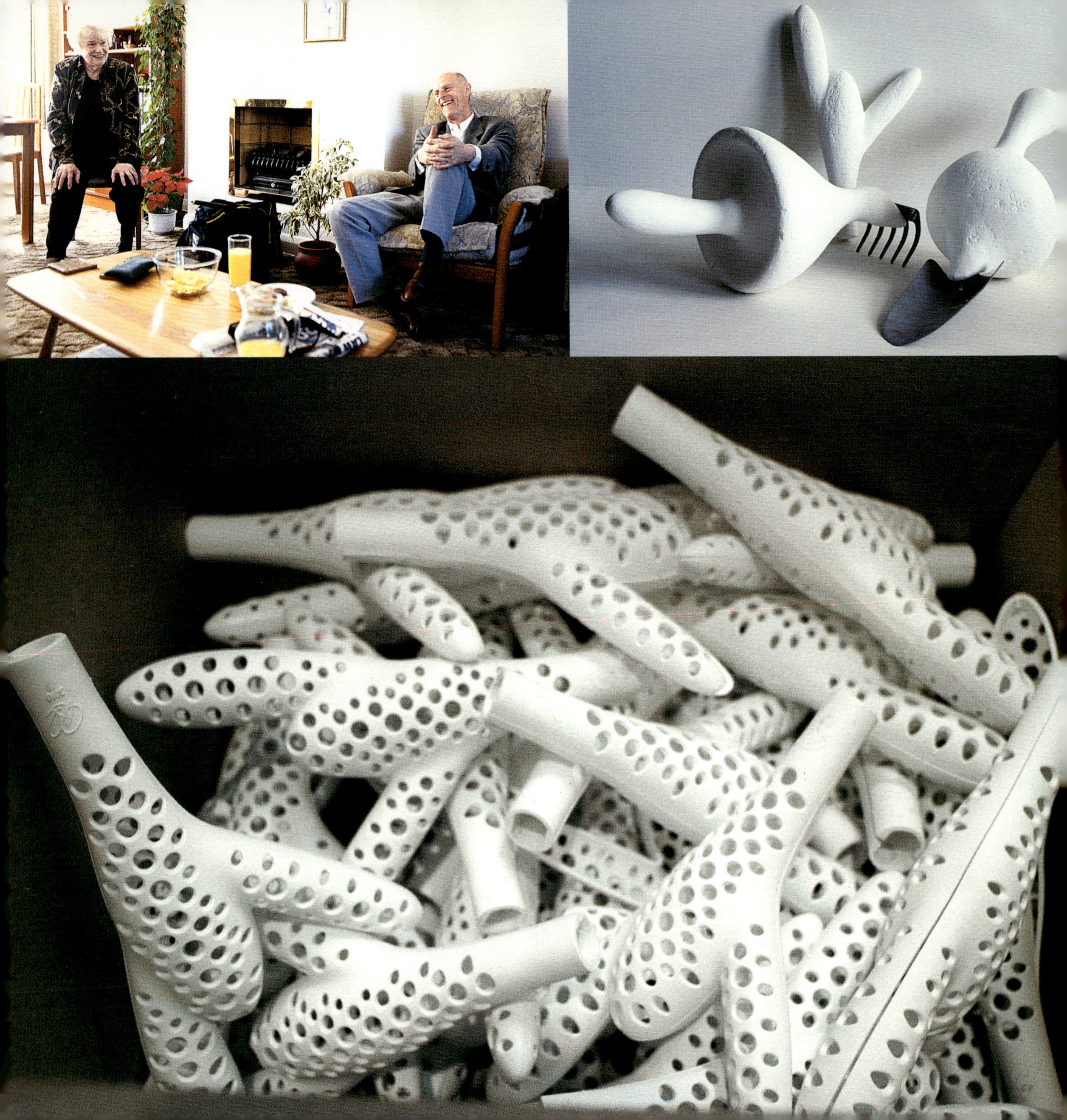

Tony Cragg

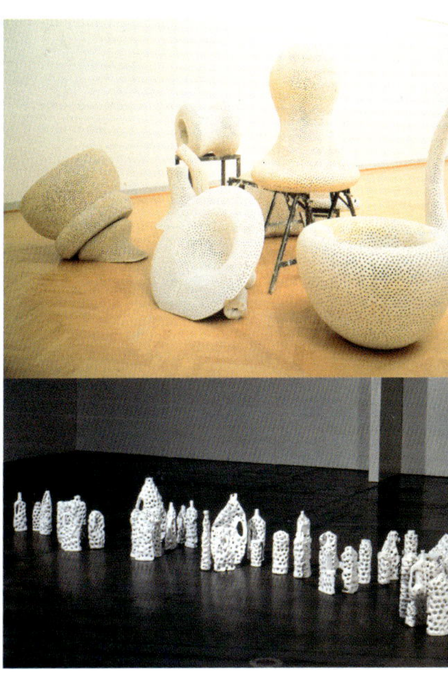

FORMINIFERA, 1991
PLASTER, EPOXY RESIN
COURTESY LISSON GALLERY

FORMINIFERA, 1989
PLASTER (32 PARTS)
COURTESY LISSON GALLERY

Colin Painter: Tony Cragg, whose studio is in Germany, was the first of the nine sculptors to make a household visit. He established a good rapport with Edna and Denis – to the extent that he took the trouble to visit their home again in the middle of a busy schedule on a brief visit to London to install his work at the Royal Academy.

Cragg made a number of proposals along with the garden tools. A dust-pan and brush and a baby's bottle were among them. Edna had announced that she was to become a grandmother for the first time and Cragg gave priority to the baby's bottle which was based on the form of a human breast. However, since Homebase do not stock baby products that idea was not developed. Edna's interest in gardening led to a more productive outcome in the form of the garden tools.

Part of Cragg's reasoning was characteristically both droll and sound. He always loses his garden tools – so why not make garden tools that you can leave in the earth when you finish working? The handles will contribute to the garden as sculpture; the tools will be readily visible when next needed.

He produced solid models for three tools (in the event, two were developed), the handles of which were intended to be manufactured as hollow. Sketches indicated the approximate nature and distribution of holes in the handles.

Paul Moore and Carl Jones of Spear and Jackson were excited about the prospect of realizing the tools despite the very short time-scale. The biggest task was to mass produce the handles in injection-moulded plastic. There followed a hectic period during which Cragg exchanged e-mails and faxes with Jones and Moore to inform the process of computer imaging being undertaken by Mark Forth of Delcam UK.

Tony Cragg has said that he wants his work to generate a dialogue with people as an object – not as a special category called 'sculpture'. These garden tools cleverly undermine distinctions between sculpture and functional objects.

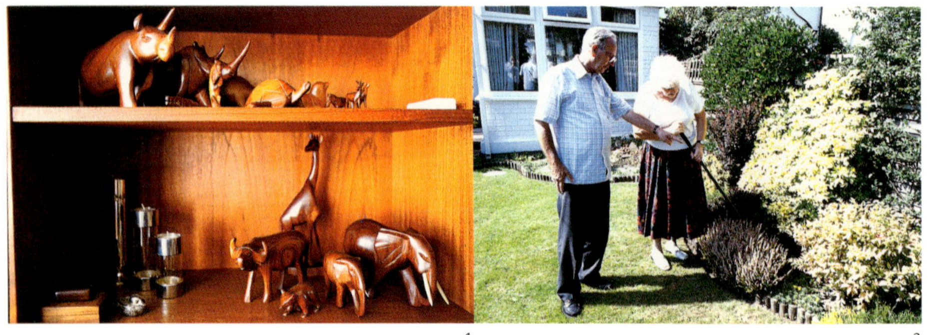

1 PART OF EDNA'S COLLECTION OF WOODEN ANIMALS

2 DENIS AND EDNA IN THEIR GARDEN

3 TONY CRAGG AND ASSISTANTS IN HIS STUDIO IN GERMANY
WITH SKETCHES OF PROPOSALS

4 HANDLES IN INJECTION MOULDING MACHINE

5 JIM MALIN, CARL JONES AND PAUL MOORE WITH HANDLES AT
SPEAR AND JACKSON

Edna and Denis Day

DENIS: I don't have much to do with what's displayed around the house. Edna takes the initiative on that kind of thing. I just have my collection of trophies from playing bowls. My greatest achievement was to be runner-up in the Club championship. I never made it to be champion. I also collect models of old-fashioned vehicles and I'm a member of the Lledo model club.

EDNA: A picture doesn't have to be on canvas does it? It can be in your mind. I have a couple of pictures like this. One is a picture of the Matterhorn. We were on holiday in Zermatt with my son Paul and his wife. We sat in a café looking towards the Matterhorn and the mist cleared – a truly memorable sight. The other one I have in mind is a sculpture in Geneva outside the Red Cross Museum. It's a group of people without facial expressions. They seemed so lost. It was pouring with rain and the stone changed colour. I found it very emotional and it made me cry.

EDNA: When I think about it many of the things around us here have a story behind them. Most of them have been given to us. We spent our honeymoon in Ventnor on the Isle of Wight and when one of my sons visited Amsterdam with his wife they came across an old print of Ventnor and bought it for us. That makes it special . . . I also like wood and we have a collection of carved animals and a rather special bowl made by Philip, our youngest son.

EDNA: I love the garden and think of it as an extension of the house. I spend a great deal of time in it and can't imagine not having one. It's very formal and tidy – I guess that's me! As soon as the leaves are down I really want to pick them up. I do like things to be orderly but I've found that life is not like that – it's not to order. I try, in my mind, to put things into neat little boxes but find that there's a lot more to be found outside the boxes.

EDNA: We go to Switzerland to visit my son and his wife. The rock in the front garden is there because it's shaped like the Matterhorn. To me it is Paul; it is Sylvia; it's us going to Switzerland; and it's there in my front garden.

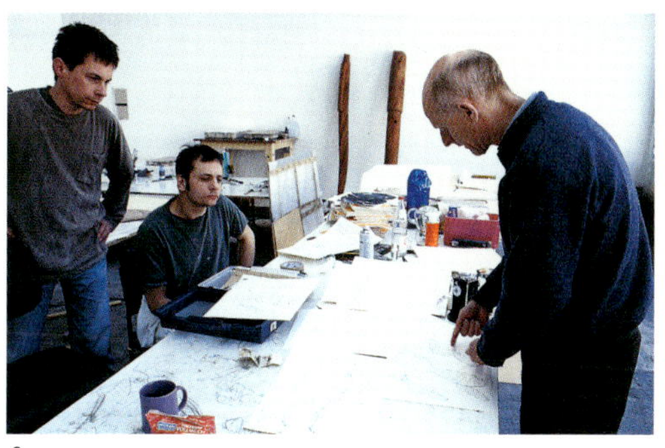

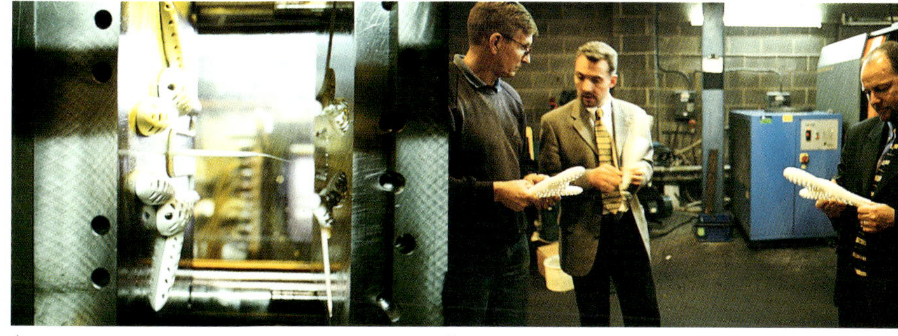

3

4

5

Tony Cragg

I've been saying for years that the utilitarian object – design – has nothing to do with sculpture making. But it did occur to me that I'd never actually put it to the test so this seemed a good opportunity to do exactly that.

> Working for mass production does force you into an economic elegance. There are lots of things you can't do because of economic constraints.

Visiting Edna and Denis gave me a real context to imagine while thinking about the work. I thought about what I would like to see out of their window. Edna brought a great deal of care and attention to the garden. It was an important space for her.

> Anybody gardening is only concerned with the aesthetic quality of it – whether it's to do with how beautiful the flowers are or how beautiful the produce is. You would expect to apply equally stringent aesthetic criteria to the tools you're using.

One difficulty was that once I'd decided on an approach in principle, I imagined the whole world being changed. I imagined the flower-pots, the wheelbarrow – a unique one-off of everything. On the one hand it is unlimited and on the other hand there are the requirements of mass production which, in making sculpture, I never experience. Obviously there is always a budget but it's really the last thing. It's a lower priority.

> I didn't want to make 'arty' tools but I like the idea of making sculptural tools. Something
> I've always criticized is the way that designed objects, useful objects, get pared down to an

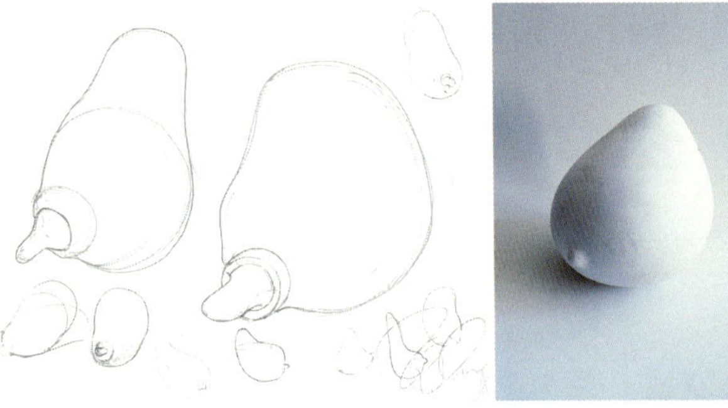

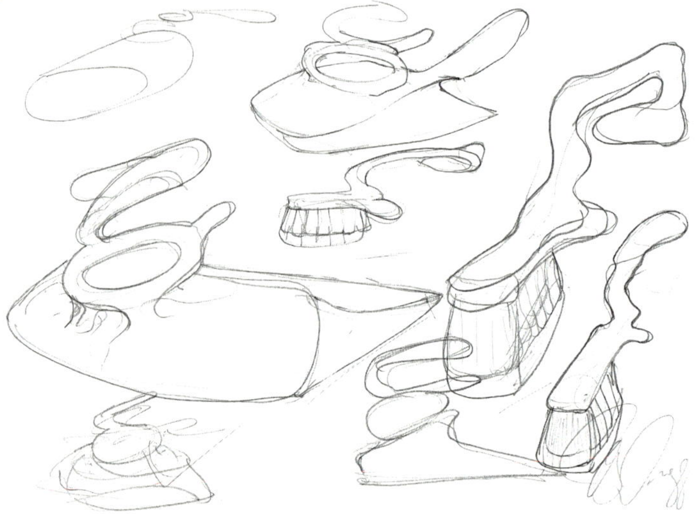

1

2

economic minimum. That's definitely not the case with these. They're actually expensive and I mean that in terms of form as well as the obvious higher production costs and subsequent selling price compared with other garden tools.

It is a modernist cliché, that art has to be challenging or disturbing. That is not the point. Art is experiential. Art offers new experiences that give us a bigger, better framework of references and, at the end of it, makes us happier in our lives and therefore fitter to survive. When art is challenging it has to have a positive, optimistic effect for the experiencer. An artist looks into something, learns about it and then makes something as a result of the learning. That will always be something unique.

These tools will inevitably have an effect. The world is full of boring, normal things – the standard issue. Anything that comes to a different solution is already offering a modified framework and is already offering the possibility for people to think differently and be different.

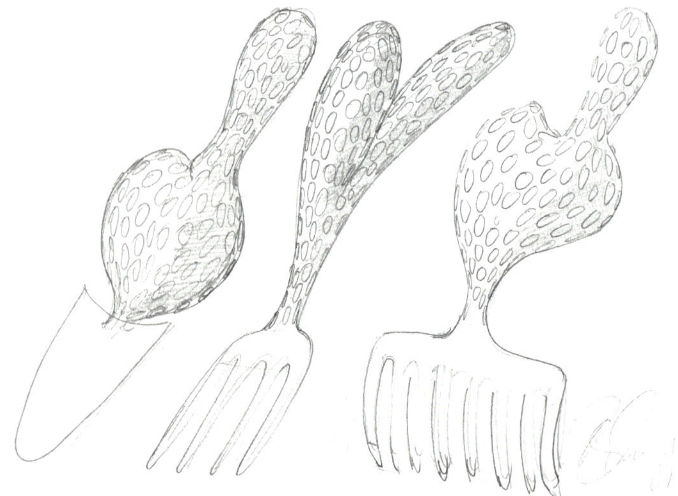

3

4

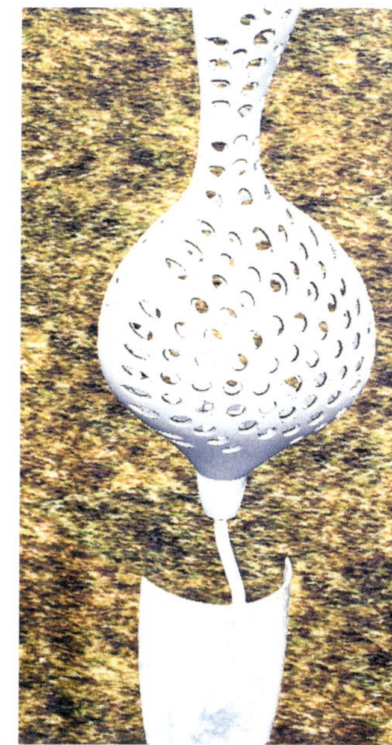

FINAL PROTOTYPES OF GARDEN TOOLS

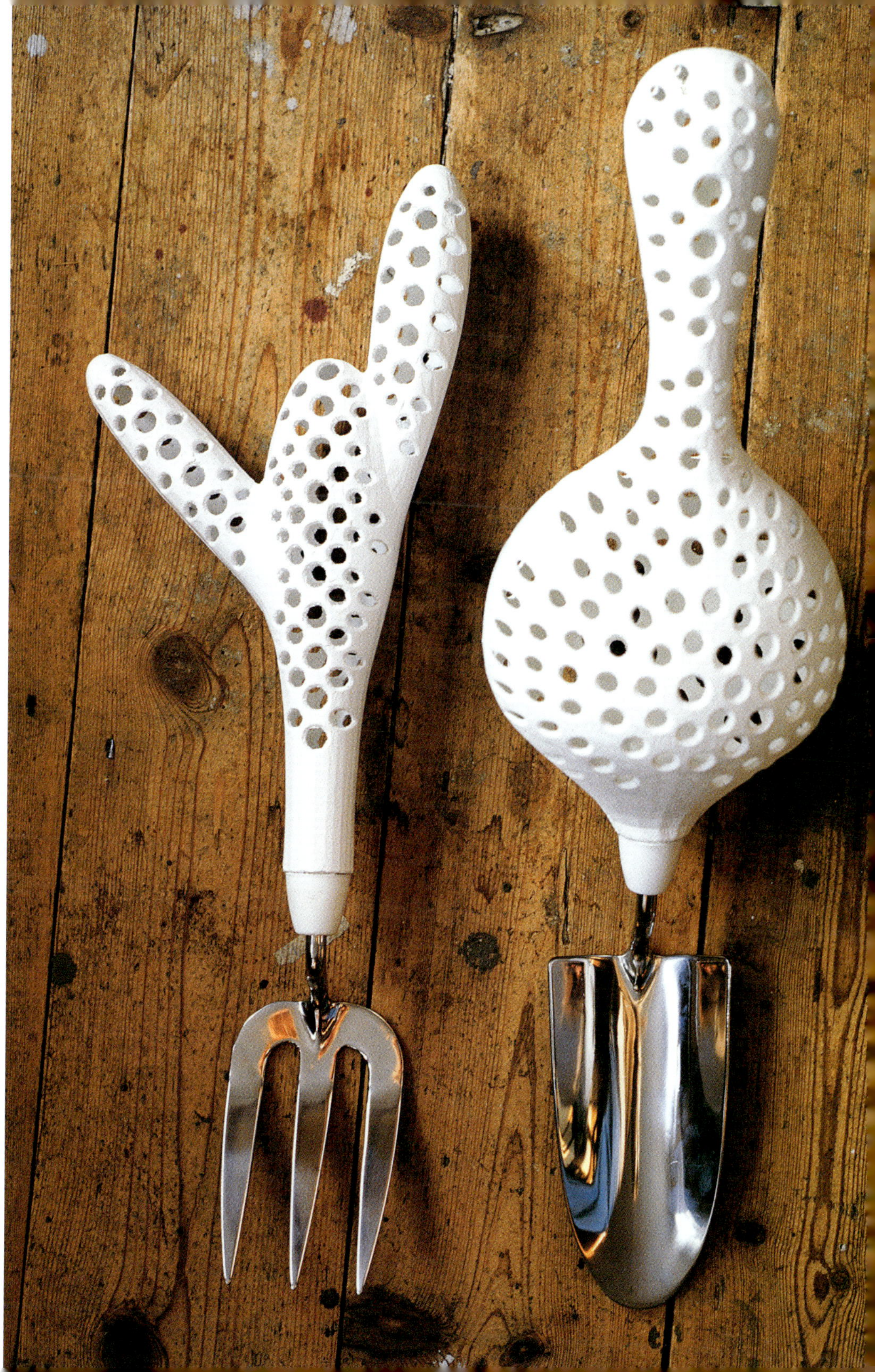

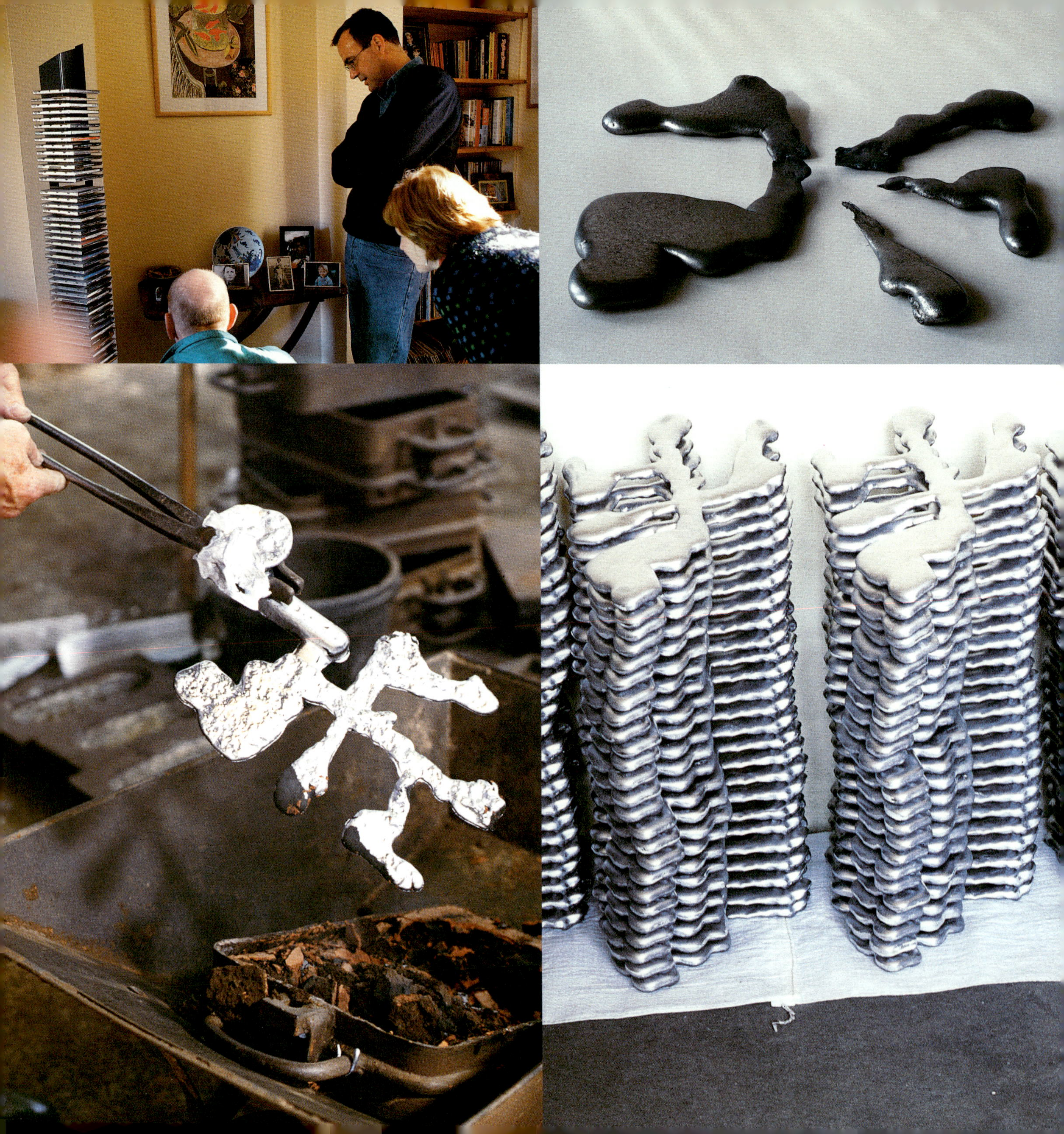

Richard Deacon

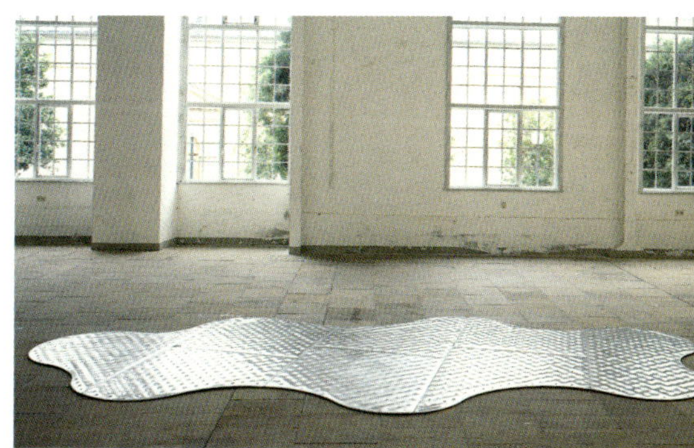

WHAT COULD MAKE ME FEEL THIS WAY (B), 1993
STAINLESS STEEL, TOKYO INTERNATIONAL FORUM
INSTALLATION: ORANGERIE, HERRENHÄUSER GARTEN, HANNOVER

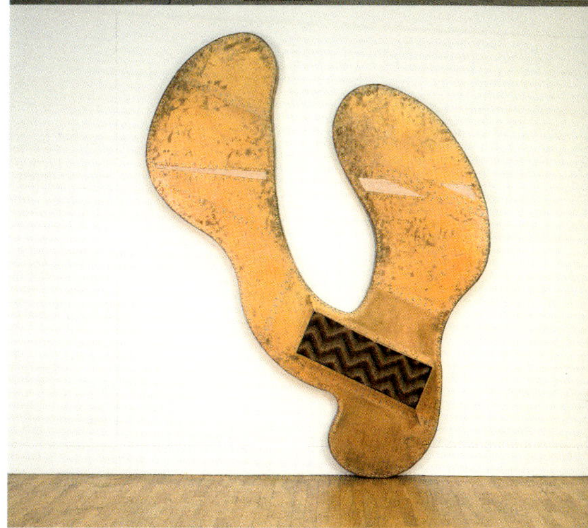

THE BACK OF MY HAND NO. 6, 1987
BRONZE, SATIN, SPONGE
PRIVATE COLLECTION, LOS ANGELES

Colin Painter: All the artists, inevitably, brought to the project their existing priorities and values. Arguably, all of them made things which were recognizably theirs. Richard Deacon appeared most readily to absorb the requirements of the project into the pulse and nature of his existing practice, accommodating them in a measured way.

He had things in common with the Mills – for example his own childhood years spent in British colonial life, well-remembered and significant. He presented several physical prototypes following his visit to their home. Practical realities of potential mass production, coupled with his insightful take on 'the souvenir', were formative in deciding on the aluminium fragments as the way forward.

Following Deacon's close instructions, 'Rob' Robinson, who runs the G.H. Plumber & Co. foundry in West Molsey, took on the task of combining the fragments as a single sculpture cast in aluminium. Like Deacon he proceeded apparently without change of stride, though he had never mass produced a sculpture before. His expertise lay in casting shapes to order – pieces of piping, motor-cycle parts – all of them sculptural if not sculpture. He didn't say so but I sensed that Deacon identified with the down-to-earth ambience of Rob's foundry.

Of the objects produced by the nine artists, Deacon's is one of the most uncompromisingly insistent on its identity as sculpture. It eschews practical use – even though it was soon seen by some as a potential trivet. Its total lack of fixed orientation – you can hang it any way up, any way round, lie it on the flat either way up – demands the participation of the 'spectator' in a rich and evocative way.

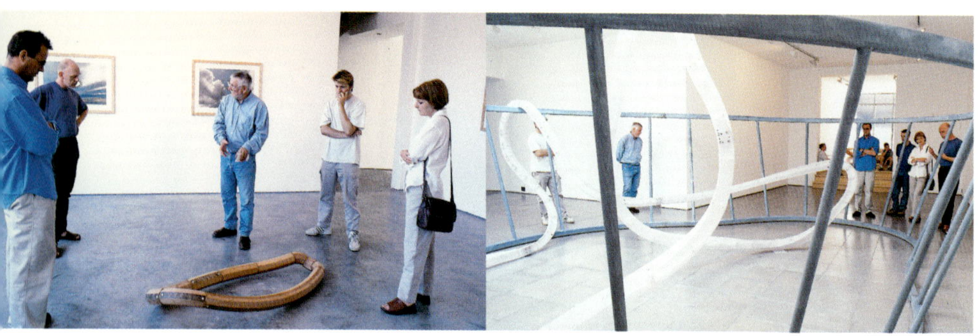

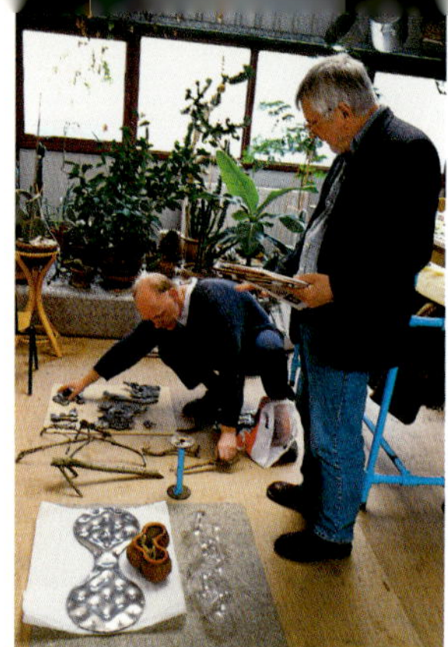

1

2

3

Dominic and **Beth Mills** (three sons aged between eight and fourteen)

BETH: We started off with all the things Dominic's mother gave us. It was all heavy Victorian.

DOMINIC: You get things that are passed on from your family or whoever. You live with it and eventually you decide that you don't actually really like it or it just doesn't fit.

BETH: We've each hung on to particular things. Our tastes are very different in many ways. I've clung on to the paintings of Dominic's ancestors. I love them.

DOMINIC: I don't like them because I find them dark and depressing – a bit overbearing. I didn't have any real relationship with the people in them. I identify more with the picture of the home I lived in for a while as a child. It's a classic old colonial house in Penang, an island off Malaysia. My father worked there and lived a very comfortable Empire-type lifestyle.

BETH: I used to work for Lufthansa so I was able to fly a lot. A number of things I have are souvenirs from my travels. Things from Burma, Peru, Bolivia, Zambia, India, Malaysia.

DOMINIC: I think the things you have around you should relate to the shape and scale of the room. On the chimney breast in the living room, for example, we have a picture which replicates the shape of the chimney breast above the mantelpiece. You need a big picture there but it also has to be the right shape . . . I like things to be harmonious with the room.

BETH: For me the things around us in our home are experiences. Looking at them means something and makes me feel something. I am not interested in them as objects so much as what they trigger off.

DOMINIC: We've got three children and they make a lot of noise – as children do. All the things in the living room are peaceful and lower the pace. They're restful to look at.

BETH: It takes courage to make choices and put things on the walls. We have different priorities in different rooms. In the kitchen I'm more concerned that things should work than I am with their appearance.

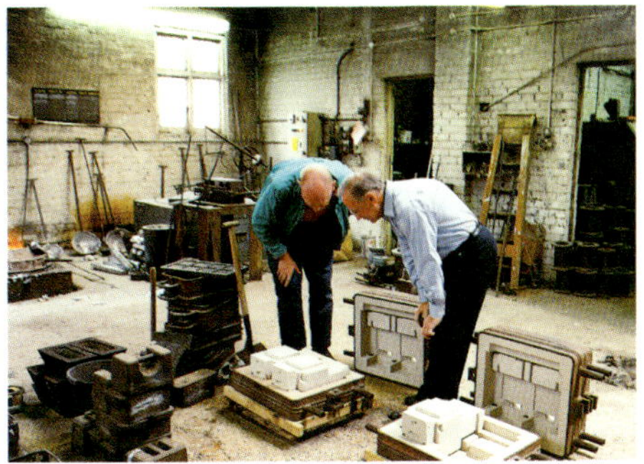

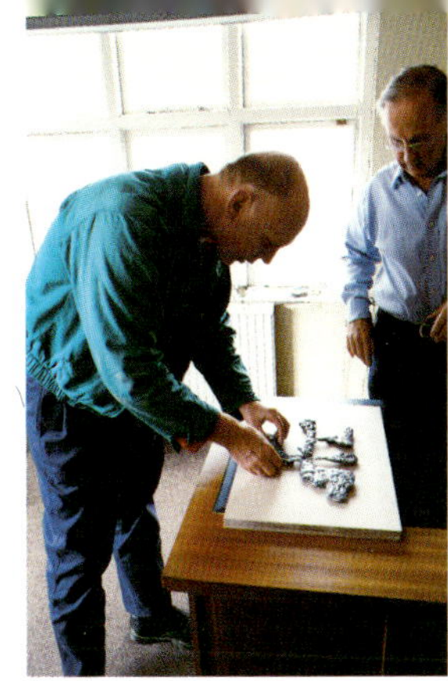

4

5

Richard Deacon

Mass production automates an element of anonymity that already exists in the making of my work. Hand making is an important part of it but if a thing is put together with screws it doesn't matter whether it's me who puts the screws in or anybody else. The expressive mark doesn't interest me. I'd like my sculpture to be repairable in the same way as a car. You should be able to take off a bit and put a new bit on it.

> Starting in the Mills's home was influential. They have souvenirs of an interesting sort. The souvenir is an intriguing class of object. It contains memories, or associations, but it doesn't necessarily resemble them. It's a reminder rather than a representation.

I found a burnt-out car in a wood. It was a shocking experience because it was a pleasant piece of woodland and a very violent act had taken place. Molten metal had dripped on to leaf mould under trees, taking an impression as it cooled – fragments which were smooth on one side, textured on the other. The sculpture is a souvenir made from the fragments. It can be imagined as either liquid or solid, land or water. I like the way this changes the surroundings.

> One way of looking at the piece is to think of it as a map. On one side it's the sea. On the other side it's the land/ground. Each of those interpretations changes the reading of the spaces around. When the map is of the sea, the surroundings are solid and when it is the land, the surroundings are liquid.

As a child I was anxious that disaster might befall in the night. I kept an escape kit under my bed. The kit contained string, a knife, a half-crown and a map. The map was one I'd invented but I knew that if

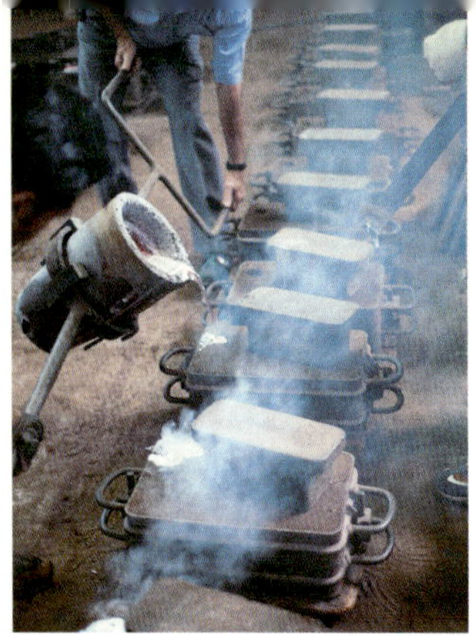

1

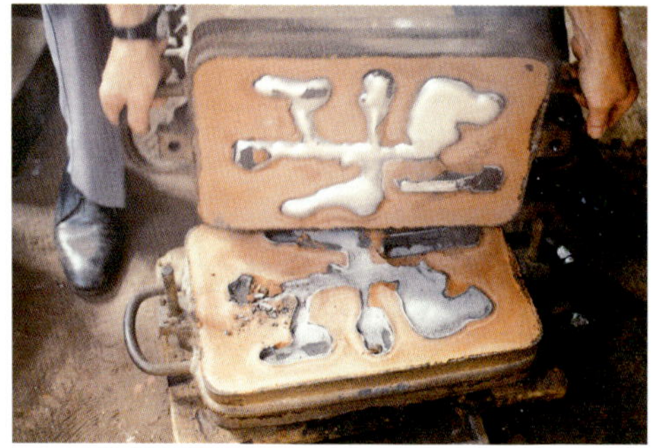

2

you were going somewhere a map was kind of useful. It was a treasure island kind of map. Reflecting on why it is that children draw maps of this kind, I realized that the map represented another place but the 'otherness' was defined by boundary. So a street-map wouldn't do. The 'A – Z', for example, is continuous and goes off the edge of the page.

> The audience for what I do is very limited in terms of acquiring the objects I make. There are extremely strong price constraints and there are also inhibitions to do with entering galleries and museums. Most people who see my work are not potential consumers. They go to it for the sake of a particular kind of experience.

The idea of an unlimited edition is interesting but in order for it to work there has to be a means of distribution in the same way there is for books, videos and films, etc. That means of distribution isn't going to be a gallery. One has to take a risk with context. The 'white cube' gallery is a defining context for looking at contemporary art. If you step outside that you do take a risk. But I shop at Homebase and I think it will be interesting to find things like this there.

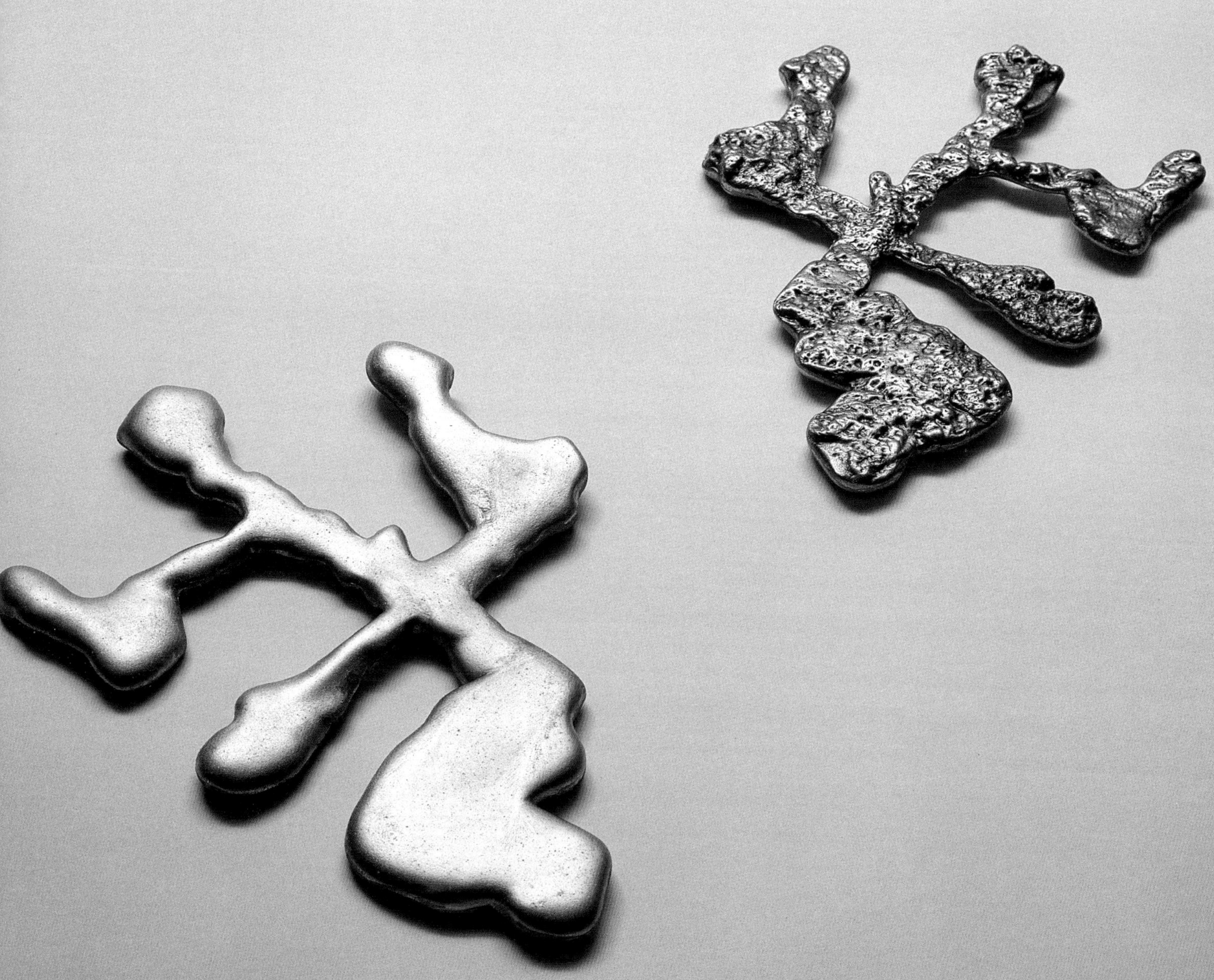

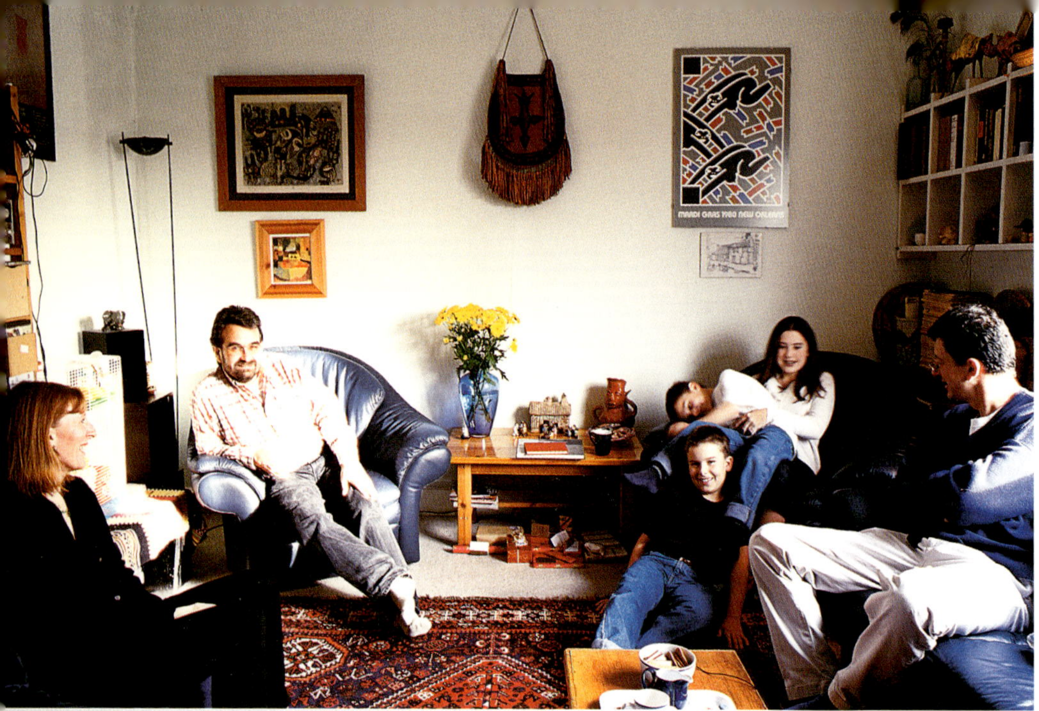

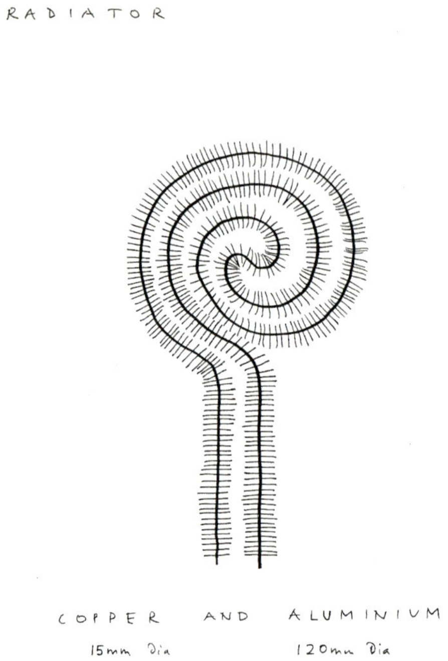

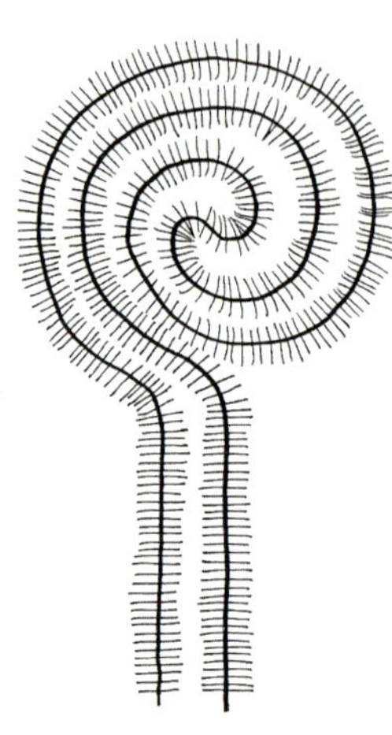
RADIATOR
COPPER AND ALUMINIUM
15mm Dia   120mm Dia

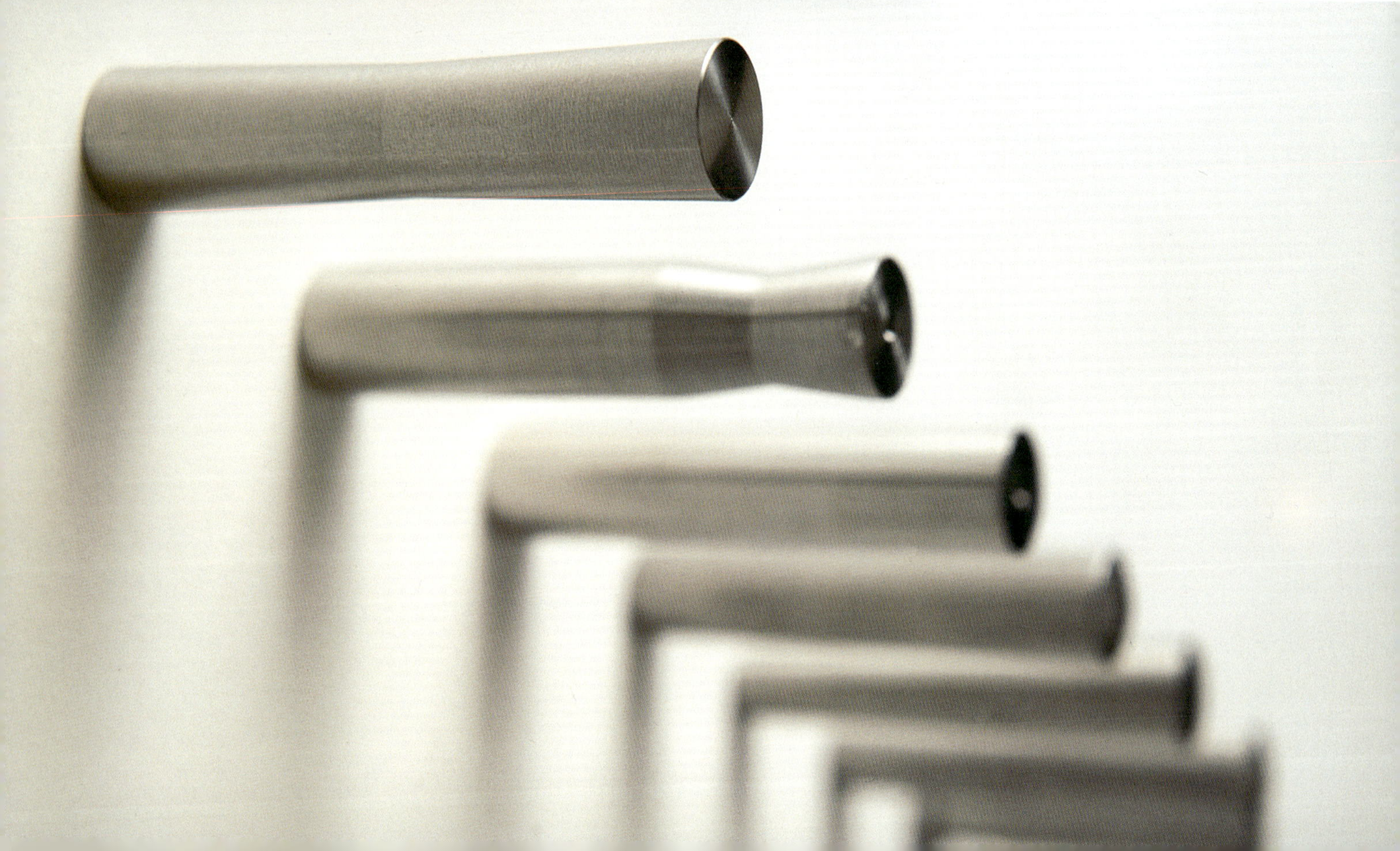

Antony Gormley

Colin Painter: From the start Antony Gormley expressed a strong wish to make something that was integral to the structure of the home. That ambition seems consistent with the way in which his familiar figures emphasize connectedness with site – ground, wall, ceiling or sea. Though he rejected the notion, I perceived the possible implication that moveable domestic objects might be thought relatively trivial, incompatible with the silent seriousness – the sense of stature, permanence and continuity – in his sculpture.

Using his own family at the breakfast table as a sounding board, a range of possibilities, including a heated bedside rug, were considered but the idea of a radiator emerged as favourite. Some time was spent in trying to realize that idea. The drawings were elegant, the proposals fascinating but, in the event, the deadlines imposed by the project made it impossible to solve all the functional problems associated with producing a reliable and useful radiator in the time available. It may well be a project for the future.

The ultimate peg evolved through a number of prototypes. Gormley was unusual in the project in that he carried out negotiations with the manufacturer entirely by fax and telephone – drawings and instructions – with me operating as go-between with Bob Russell, Engineering Manager at Granton Ragg Ltd. in Sheffield. This proved economical since Russell was also working on Angela Bulloch's tuning fork.

Gormley's claims for his peg are modest – 'a re-invented nail' – but its simplicity asserts its own profundity which, of course, is not fully realized until the peg is fixed in a surface.

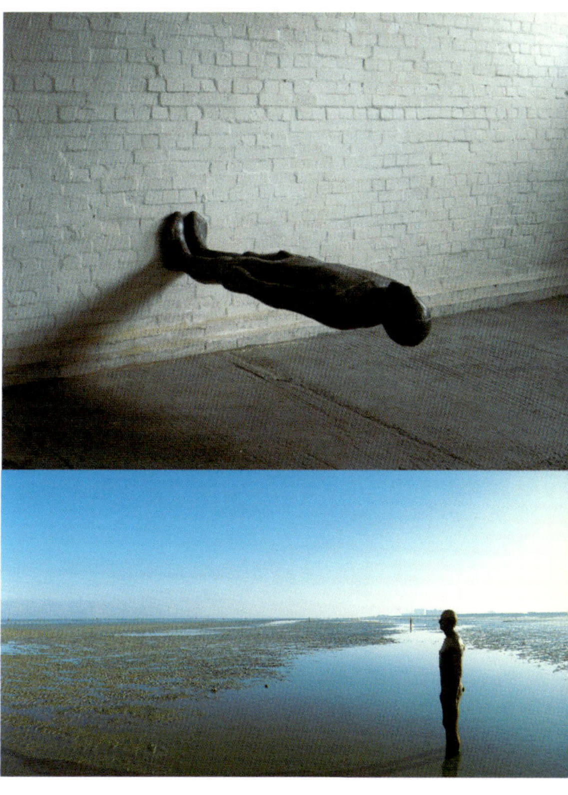

EDGE, 1985
LEAD, FIBREGLASS, PLASTER, AIR
PRIVATE COLLECTION, COURTESY JAY JOPLING, LONDON

ANOTHER PLACE, 1997
CAST IRON, 100 SOLID BODY-FORMS, CUXHAVEN, GERMANY
COURTESY GALERIE NORDENHAKE, SWEDEN

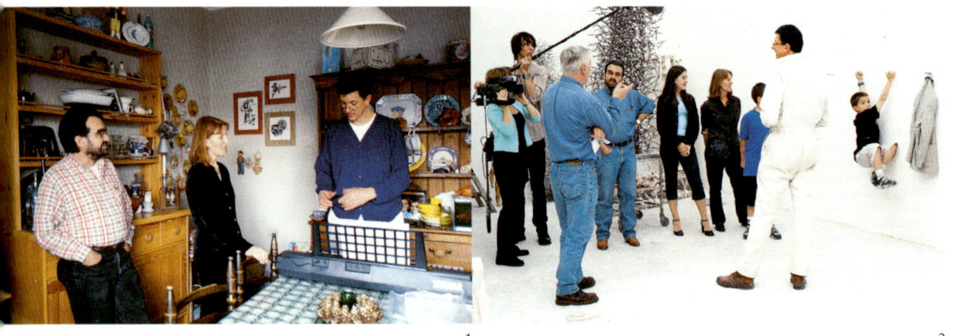

1 ANTONY GORMLEY AT THE SPRAGG FAMILY'S HOME

2 ANTONY GORMLEY BEING FILMED IN THE STUDIO
WITH THE SPRAGG FAMILY

3 ANTONY GORMLEY IN HIS STUDIO WITH A RANGE OF
PROTOTYPES

4 BOB RUSSELL TESTING THE PEG AT GRANTON RAGG LTD.

Nigel Spragg and **Philippa Direen** (two sons and one daughter aged between seven and fourteen)

PHILIPPA: In New Zealand, where I grew up, I was used to having lots of space and every now and then I feel
I'd like to be able to see a clear wall. But I also really love having things around me that remind me of
our travels and the things the kids have done – a lot of child-oriented things – like their pieces of
pottery. I tend to make the decisions about where things go. I like things to relate to the furniture and I
like groups of pictures together.

NIGEL: Travel has always been very important. It probably still would be but it's more difficult to do with the
three kids. You're more likely to acquire things in the ornamental or artistic realm when you travel.

PHILIPPA: We both take a lot of photographs. I prefer to photograph people – and especially children. In the
music room we have a wall of family photographs that I've taken. The children are just so beautiful – I
just want to capture their faces.

NIGEL: I've had an obsession with the Third World since I was tiny. I remember at secondary school being
mad about Africa. I ended up fortunate enough to go there. I even buy African stuff here. Anything else
– whether it's Asian or South American – I've obtained on my travels. I bought the saddle bag in Nigeria.
The figure in the middle is a Southern Cross. I wear a gold Southern Cross round my neck.

PHILIPPA: At the bottom of the stairs I have a group of family photographs and other related things from
New Zealand. All my ancestors were from Ireland. In the big wooden houses in New Zealand they used
to have beautifully-framed pictures of ancestors. They were photographs touched up with paint.

NIGEL: I have a lot of unusual things. There's a thing in the kitchen … it's a pin with a brass American foot-
baller on it saying, 'For Texas I will'. It was given to me by a friend who ran an antique shop because she
knew I loved Texas. It's not a particularly attractive image but I like it because it's weird.

PHILIPPA: We have a photocopy of a drawing by a friend of the house we owned in France. We sold the
house recently and the picture is very important because I loved the house very much. It's not in the
right place where it is but I wanted to have it up.

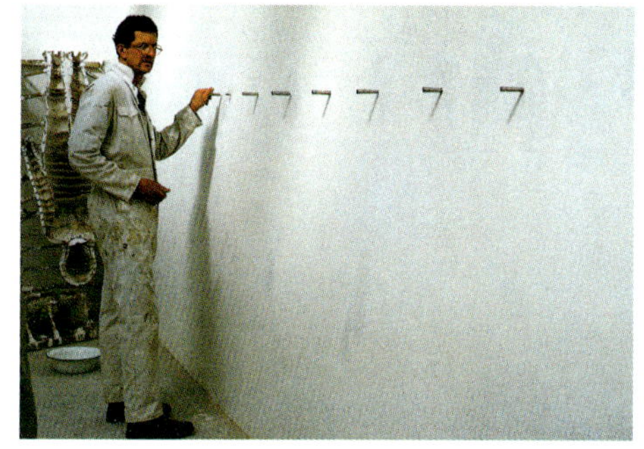

3

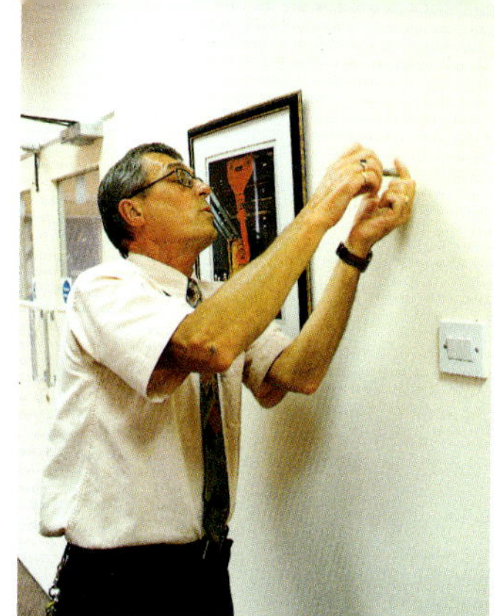

4

Antony Gormley

I welcomed the project as an attempt to make an infiltration into the domestic lives of a wide public, but I also liked the opportunity to think about domestic life: those conditions that surround and support us. In a curious way the domestic realm is not immediately associated with art, but a kitchen is a studio, a living room is a studio. When you have a conversation with somebody you are using the space in another person's mind as a place for testing out ideas – that is like a studio.

> Visiting the Spragg household was seminal. Their flat was full of things hanging on walls that might not have been thought of as belonging on walls – a leather bag from Morocco or a piece of embroidered clothing from Baluchistan – relating to experiences in their lives. In the end I made this thing that supports that desire to hang things on the wall. I've re-invented a nail.

My nail, or peg, tries to do all the common jobs of a coat hook but also does the job that the nails on the wall in the Spragg's house were doing, which was to act as a support for the isolation of objects which could then be looked at in a different way. I want it to act as an interface between the blankness of the wall and the particularity of the object.

> For me it seemed the invitation of the project was to put art at the service of life and that implied a movement towards the position of craft. In other words responding to human need first. I think art's most important purpose is to challenge, not to support. What I have responded to is the need to make life more liveable. This is a functional object which responds to a particular need in the same way that a cup or a plate or a pair of trousers does. It's just a place to put things.

From the beginning I wanted to make something that was integral to
the structure of a building, but I'm not sure if I succeeded because
when the peg has nothing hanging on it you get a strong sense of a
thing in space. I hope that's useful in itself. It gives the eye something
to fix on – so it's a kind of eye hook as well as a coat hook.

The essence of sculpture is best expressed by a bullet or a
bomb, an object that is perfectly complete but capable of
changing everything. The peg has a little bit of that in it.
I've always loved Walter De Maria's high energy bar. The
peg is like a high energy nail. It manages to be both aloof
and integrated. It's saying that it can be both in life and
stand apart from it.

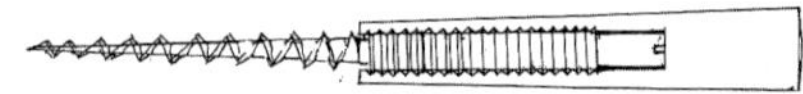

DRAWING FOR AN EARLY PROTOTYPE OF THE PEG

THE FINAL PEG WITH SCREW

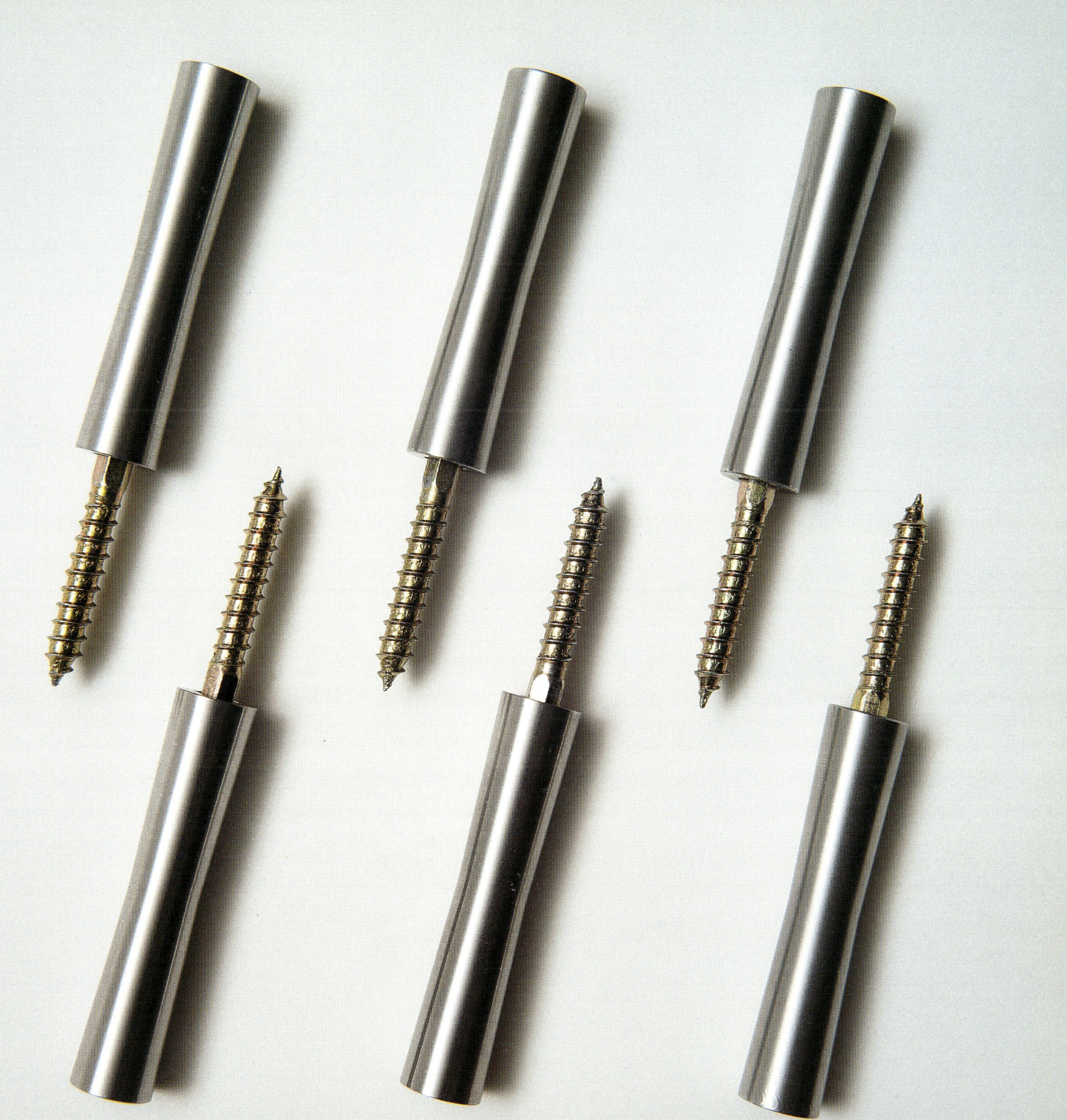

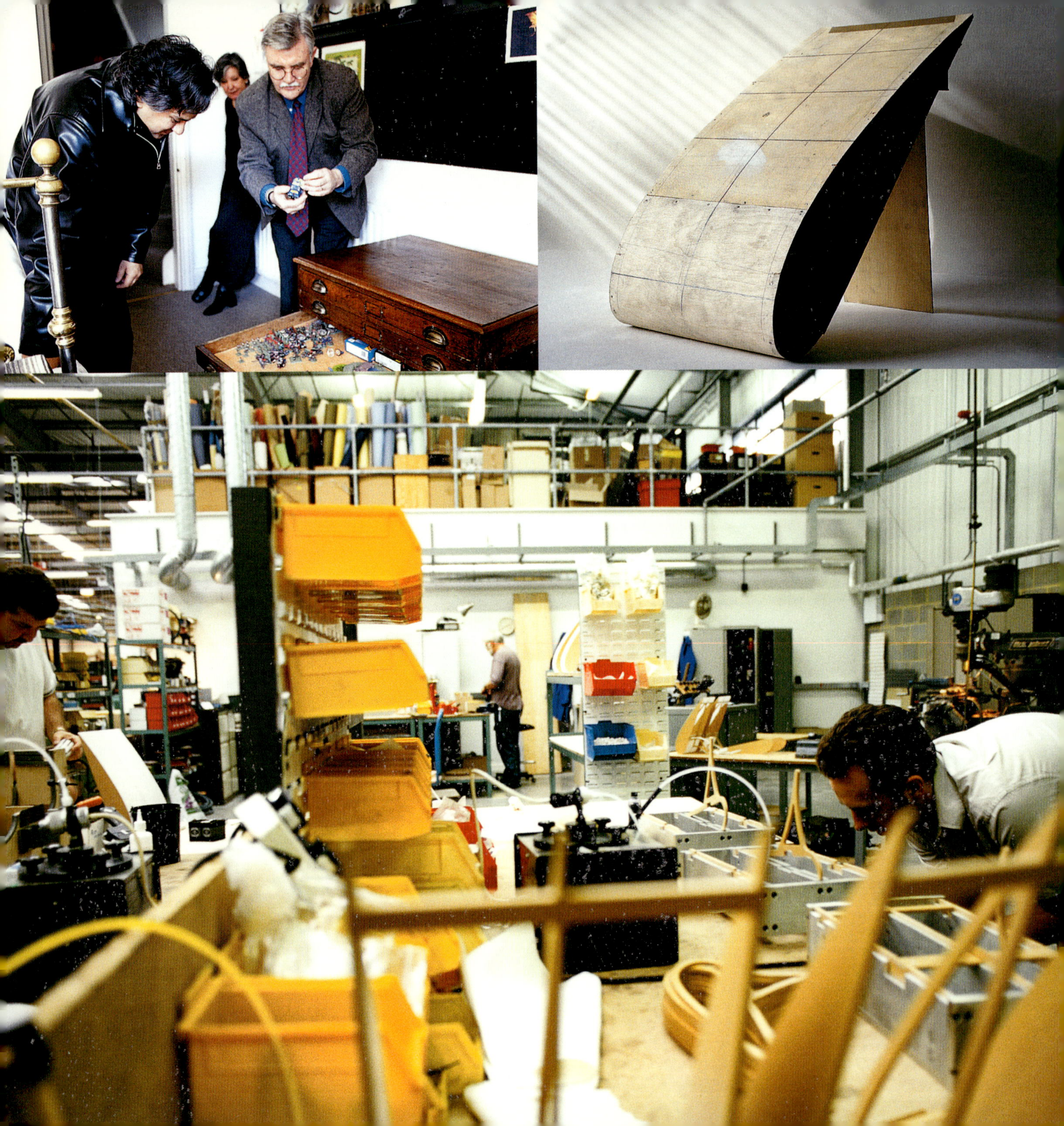

Anish Kapoor

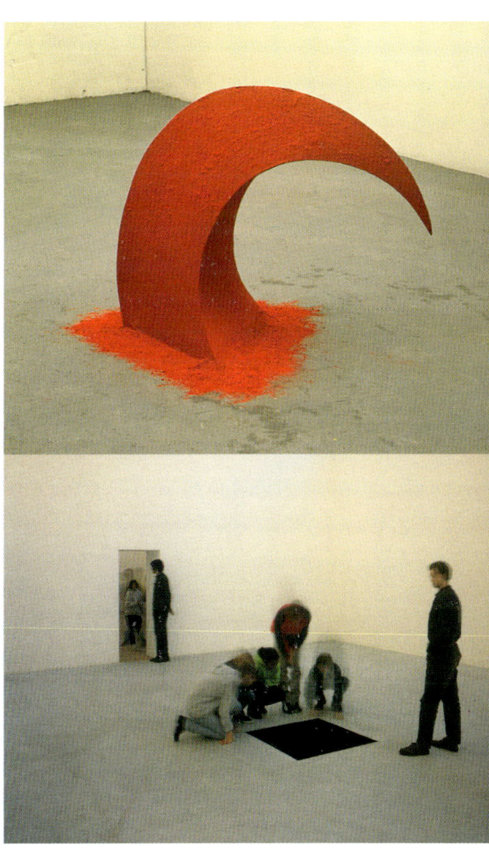

1000 NAMES, 1979–80
WOOD, GESSO, PIGMENT
COURTESY LISSON GALLERY

UNTITLED, 1996
WOOD, PIGMENT
INSTALLATION: MALMO KONTSHALL, COURTESY LISSON GALLERY

Colin Painter: As he explains later here, Anish Kapoor took some time to identify a way forward following his visit to the Jarman's. Once he had decided on a lamp, however, developments were steady, systematic and rigorous.

I took his wooden model to the Welwyn Lighting Company, which supplies lighting to Homebase, and met Mary Van Hogermeer and Phillip Lazell of the design department. Anish had given me some initial thoughts about possible materials – paper or card; an indication of colour – white; and the surfaces that might illuminate. Based on the model and these tentative ideas, Van Hogermeer and Lazell produced drawings and three or four prototypes. There followed a series of meetings, first at Welwyn Lighting and subsequently at Kapoor's studio, at which progressively modified and refined prototypes were produced and discussed.

The meetings were focused and intense. Kapoor was precise in his thoughts and the two designers were quick to pick up on his ideas. It was a fascinating interaction. Successive prototypes, testing different visual and practical solutions, were considered and superseded. At one point Kapoor took two prototypes home to live with.

The resulting lamp is an elegant embodiment of characteristics evident in Kapoor's sculpture: economy, profundity, religiosity and not a little theatre.

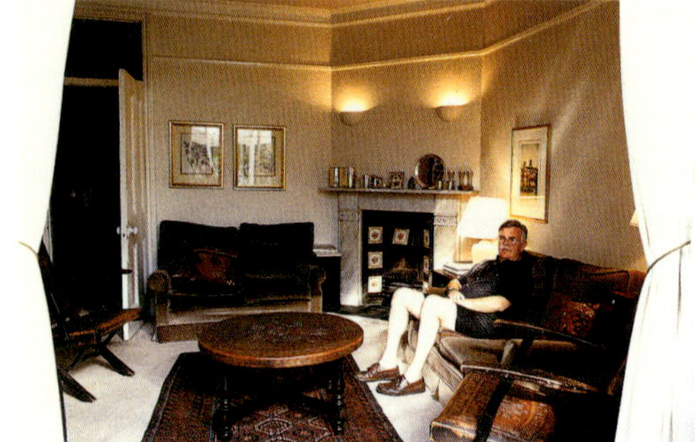

1 PAUL JARMAN IN HIS HOME

2 ANISH KAPOOR WITH FIRST GENERATION PROTOPYES AT THE WELWYN LIGHTING COMPANY

3 MARY VAN HOGERMEER AND PHILLIP LAZELL OF THE DESIGN DEPARTMENT, WELWYN LIGHTING COMPANY, IN ANISH KAPOOR'S STUDIO WITH SECOND GENERATION PROTOTYPES

Paul and **Beatriz Jarman** (son and daughter now at university)

BEATRIZ: The things in this house mostly reflect Paul's taste. He likes Victorian clutter. When I came to England from Uruguay I brought one possession – a tea-set of my grandmother's. I just wanted a piece of my family history. I've always been the one living in a foreign country. I've realized I don't like Victorian clutter.

PAUL: I've always hankered after these old things. I'm the one who didn't have to invent a history but I need the trappings of it around me. Beatriz is a free spirit. Since my mother died we've got even more things around us. It's hard to dispose of things that belonged to people who were important to you – even if you don't particularly like them.

BEATRIZ: What you're surrounded with in your home is not necessarily what would be your first choice if you had a free hand. It's what's happened to you … and it keeps ruling what you're going to have next. You've got these lamp shades so you can't have a sculpture like that because it would clash. Very often your choice is limited by money.

PAUL: This is a very dark house and we haven't got the lighting right. We hate central lights so I put wall lights in. I thought they'd disappear. Beatriz hates them. Then in the conservatory we have a couple of horrible, copied Victorian lights. It's quite modern out there and it would be nice to have something more in keeping. I hate copies. I like my wood to be wood and my plastic to be plastic.

BEATRIZ: I think sometimes different styles can live together happily.

PAUL: Although this is a Victorian house it is not decorated in a Victorian way. The walls are mostly beige and white – more Georgian than Victorian. I like that Georgian cleanliness.

BEATRIZ: I've come to the conclusion that if I had the money I'd like to live in a loft-style apartment.

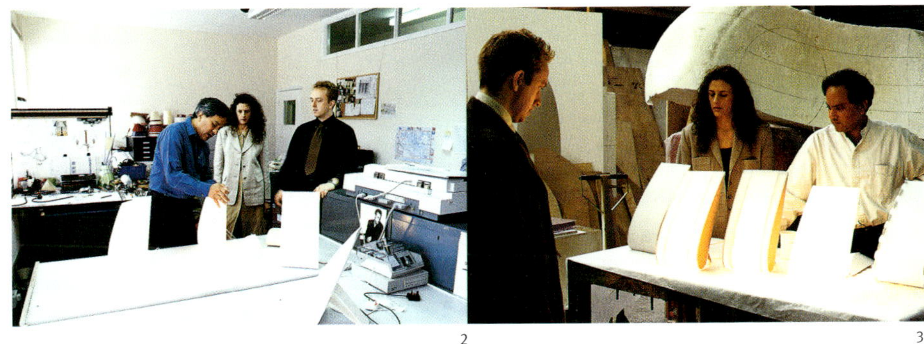

2   3

Anish Kapoor

I believe profoundly that artists make art. They don't do anything other than make art. We're not designers. But there's something very attractive about the methodology involved in so-called design.

> I started out not wanting to design something and ended up designing it thoroughly, doing everything I started out not wanting to do. I found that a very interesting process. Many things have opened up for me in terms of the product world in which I feel somewhat more comfortable as a designer than I did previously.

Having first of all had a great deal of difficulty deciding what to do and eventually going with the notion of a lamp, I found myself starting with a very clumsy feeling of what a lamp could be – a block of wood – then working towards a solution that made sense. I didn't come up with an idea – I arrived at an idea through the process of working. In many ways, of course, that's very similar to how I work in the studio. It's really the only way I can go about anything.

> Much of what I've been involved with as an artist is to do with notions of source. A lamp is a source. It's difficult to find lights in the contemporary market that are simple. I want this lamp to be based around the way an object is made rather than around the wonderful technology that's available. I see this lamp as a 'low-tech' proposition.

The team of lighting designers that I worked with took the germ of an idea and made it into a lamp. More happened in the process of our interaction than happened in my initial conception of the object. I found it to be a creative and fruitful dialogue.

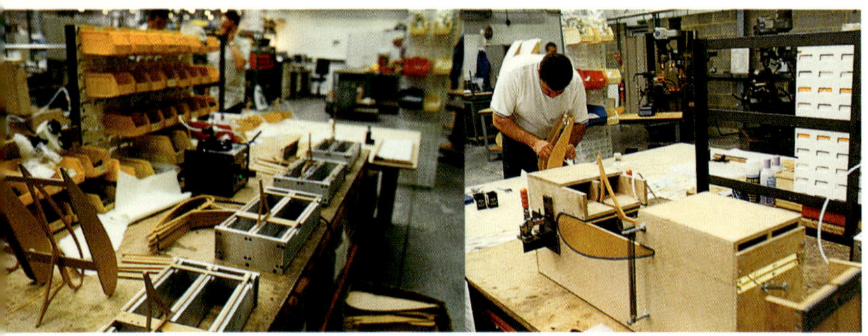

1   2

When I first started out I didn't imagine it would be possible to make something at the sort of cost involved in this project. It's been something of a revelation to be able to manufacture an object of quality for a relatively low price. I find that a very good thing. If nothing else, it motivates me to want to do that again.

I was nervous at first about having my work in a context like Homebase. Context lends so much to the way in which any object is seen. But I've come round to the idea that one can hope to work towards quality in a place that's also about popularity. The two things are not mutually exclusive.

The great lesson that history teaches us about art is that it's about connoisseurship – irrespective of radicality. To declare that we live in an age where radicality is all that matters and that connoisseurship goes out of the window makes banal the whole of the soulful process of looking. We are artists to deal with the soulful.

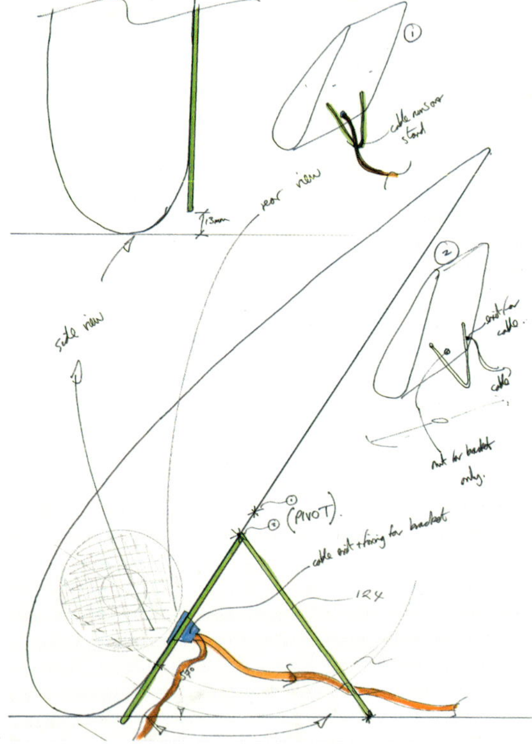

3

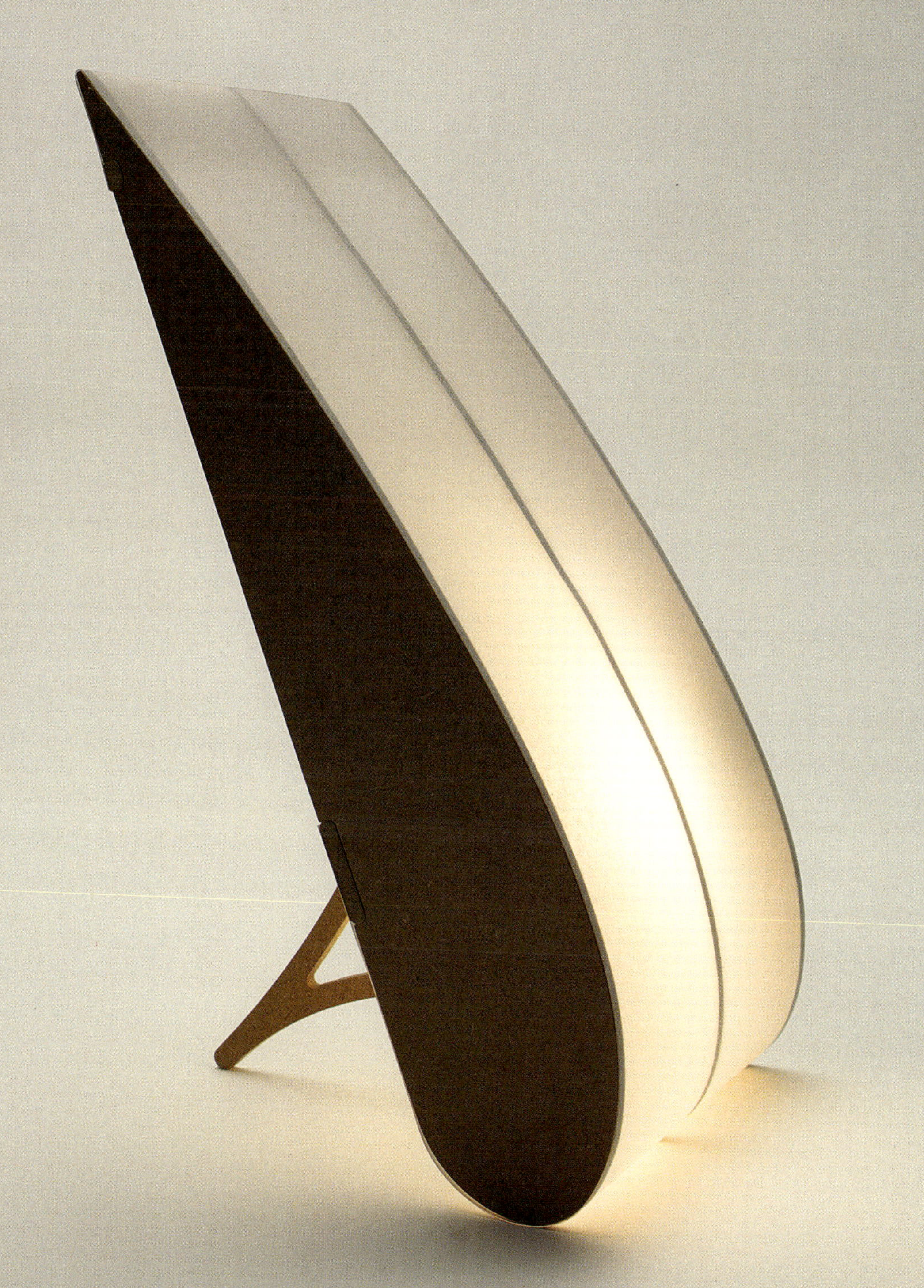

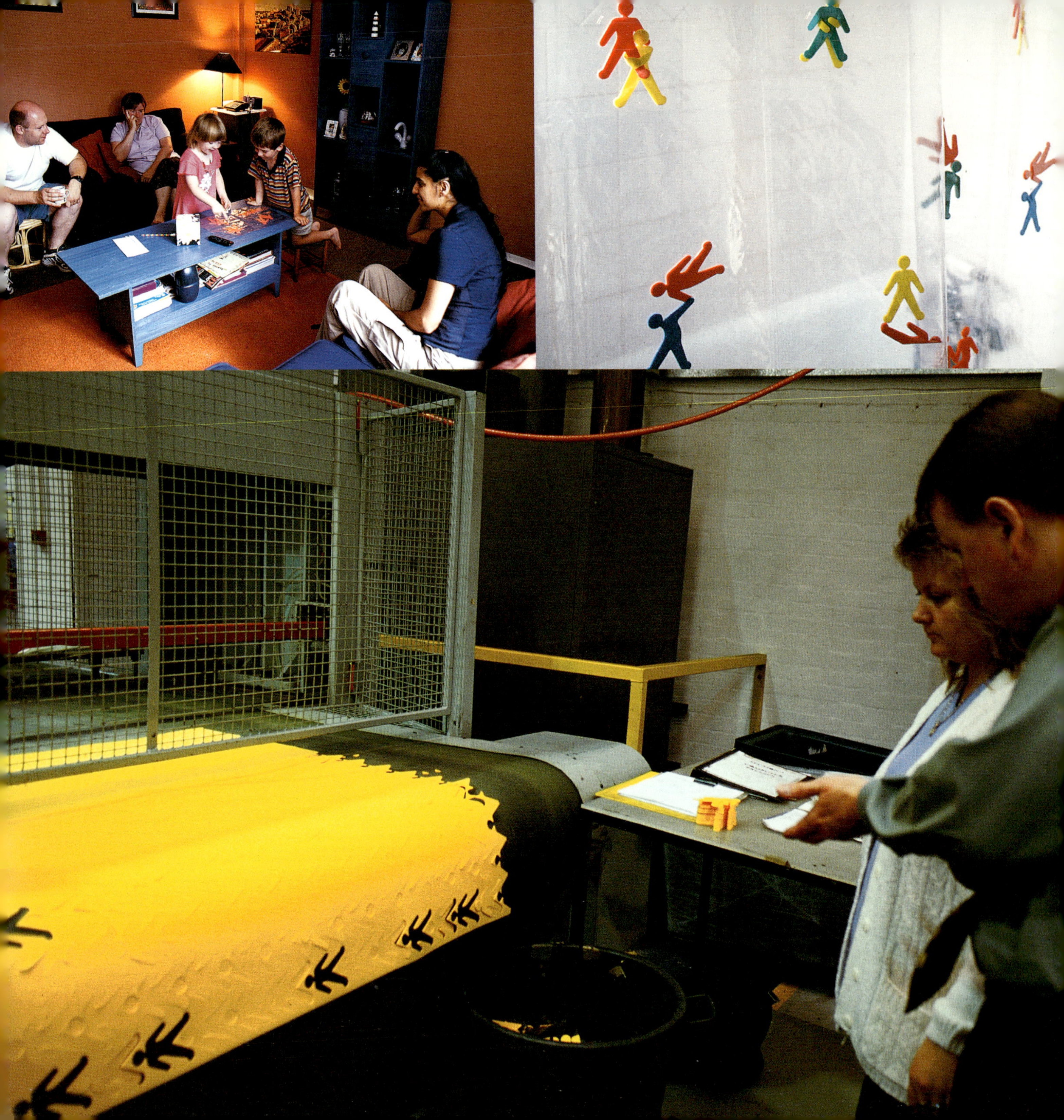

Permindar Kaur

Colin Painter: Following her visit to the Wood's flat Permindar Kaur preserved some mystery about her thoughts on the way forward. What she did declare was that she would like to explore the possibility of making something using foam rubber or plastic. A short tour of some possible manufacturers in the Midlands ended with the Stafford Rubber Company where Tom Caveney, the Managing Director, proved an imaginative and flexible collaborator.

Caveney introduced a range of plastics, foams and rubber materials and offered to listen to proposals. Nobody – except maybe the artist – knew where this might be leading. Having been sent samples of materials, Kaur announced her wish to make a shower curtain. It would involve cutting figures from coloured foam and sandwiching them in pairs between sheets of clear PVC. Having never made a shower curtain before, Caveney responded with a confident offer to do the job. Based on Kaur's diagrammatic drawings he devised ways of tooling up for the task.

Much negotiation followed – the right thickness of PVC, the method of sealing in the figures, the distribution of the figures, the colours of the figures. The result is not only a unique shower curtain but a strong and relevant extension of Permindar Kaur's preoccupations as an artist, giving existing themes in her work new potential meanings.

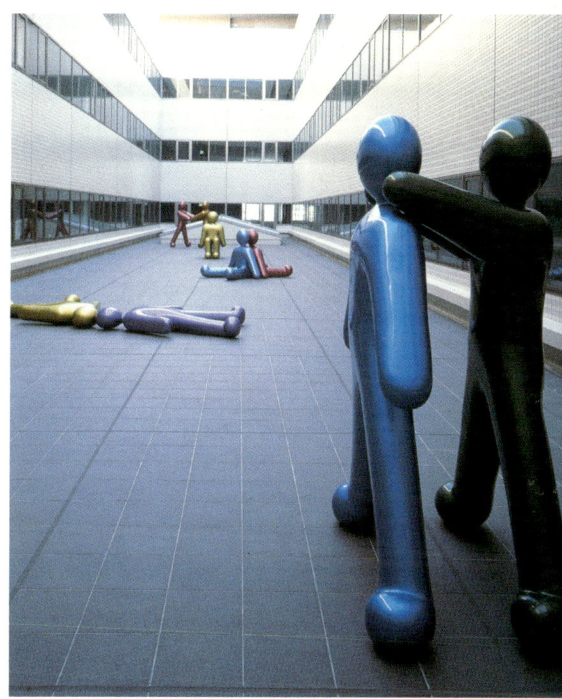

PLAYTIME, 1998–99
FIBRE-REINFORCED PLASTIC, 7 'PAIRS' OF FIGURES IN TWO COURTYARDS
HAKATA RIVERAIN ART PROJECT AT HAKATA RIVERAIN, FUKUOKA, JAPAN
COMMISSIONED BY NANJO & ASSOCIATES, TOKYO

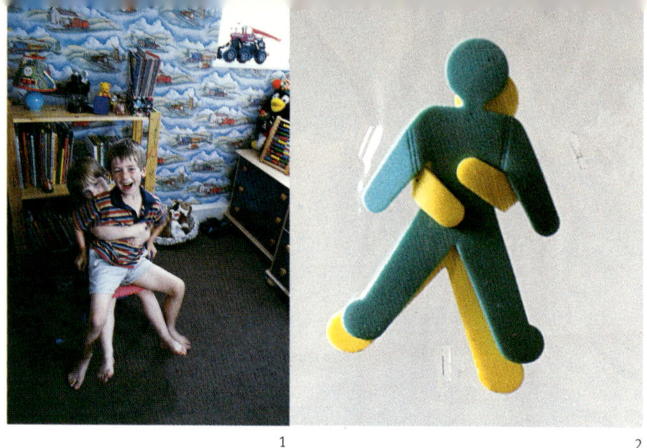

1

2

Phil and **Louise Wood** (daughter aged three and son aged five)

PHIL: We consider the colour scheme of rooms when we put things around us. The blue picture frames were
chosen to relate to the colour of the walls.

LOUISE: I like things to be ordered, not chaotic. I like to have things that are different – but not too different.
I like things that are colourful and bright. I don't think of the things around us as art – art is another
world. These are just nice pictures and things, they're what I can afford, that's what it comes down to.

PHIL: Most of our pictures are reproductions of art – I still consider them as art. But I like things that mean
something. I'd like to have all my qualifications and certificates on the walls, all my army papers and my
dad's, grandad's and great grandad's. Five generations. But Louise is not keen. If I had a study of my
own I'd put them there.

LOUISE: Those things are for photograph albums, not to go on the wall. I like to have pictures – not
photographs. You can day-dream about them, partly create them yourself, lose yourself in them and be
somewhere else.

PHIL: Although we like a lot of the same things we see them differently. They mean different things to us. I
just know that a picture reminds me of a holiday or a certain place. They're about things I've done,
places I've been. Most of the things in the cabinet are gifts, souvenirs, wedding presents.

LOUISE: The most important thing to me is the lamp standard. It's plain but slightly different at the same
time. Because of the children things have had to be kept out of reach. I'd like to buy more little objects
now that they're older.

PHIL: The most important for me is the clock which is also a ceramic hand. The ship in a bottle was in my
nan's cabinet. I always wanted to play with it but was never allowed to in case I broke it. When she died
that was one of the things I wanted 'cos I'd never been allowed to have it. So, in the end, I did have it –
and then Nicholas and Shannon came along and broke it! They bought me another one to replace it.

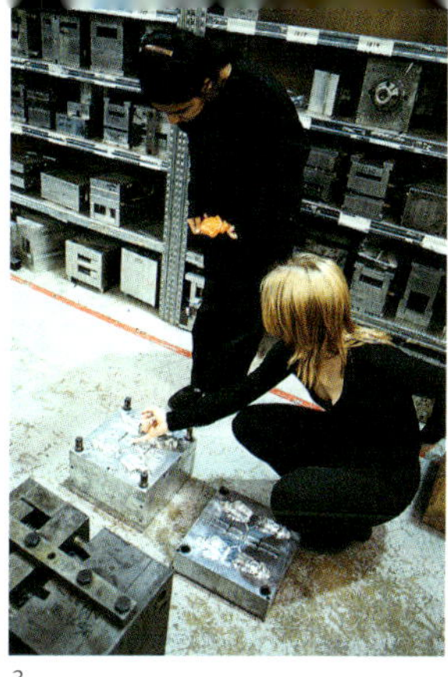

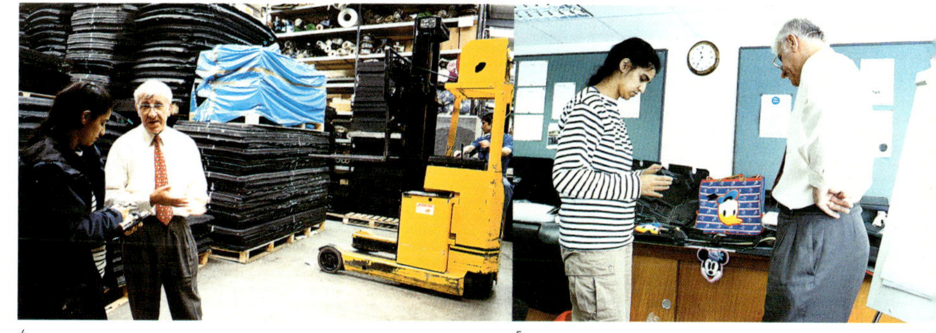

3   4   5

Permindar Kaur

This project has enabled me to work in new ways. Rather than producing a one-off which I can change and alter during its making, I had to design, through collaboration with the manufacturer, a prototype for an object for mass production.

> Making a shower curtain for the home raises questions as to the function of an art object and who it is for. This work will reach a very different audience, which I had to consider in the development of my ideas.

When people see this shower curtain, they may decide to buy it because they like the object itself, and not because they know about the artist involved in the project.

> The project offered me a choice between making a functional or art object. I considered many ideas for small unusual items. Eventually I decided to make something useful, functional, which also referenced an aspect of my work at the moment.

The relationship between figures is a recurring motif in my work. In the shower curtain the figures exist in their own worlds as private moments – both protected and revealed.

> Forms and ideas in my previous work, such as generic figures in pairs are used in the shower curtain. The relationship between the figures varies, some are positive, some are negative, most of them are quite ambiguous. In the shower curtain there are many playful elements. The work can be read on many different levels.

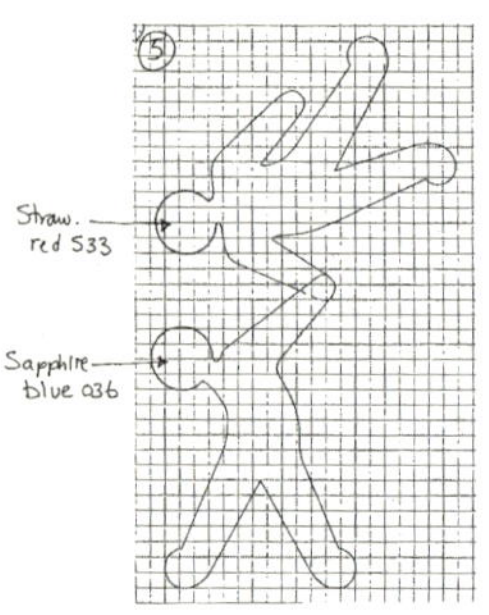
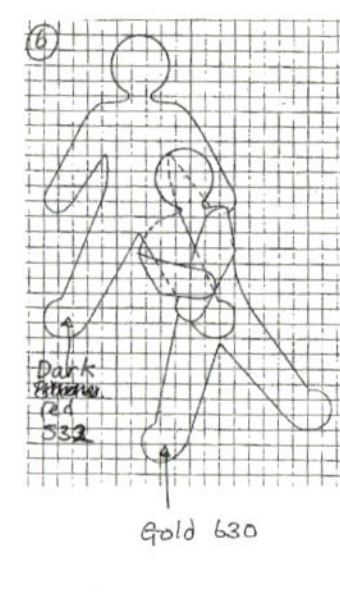

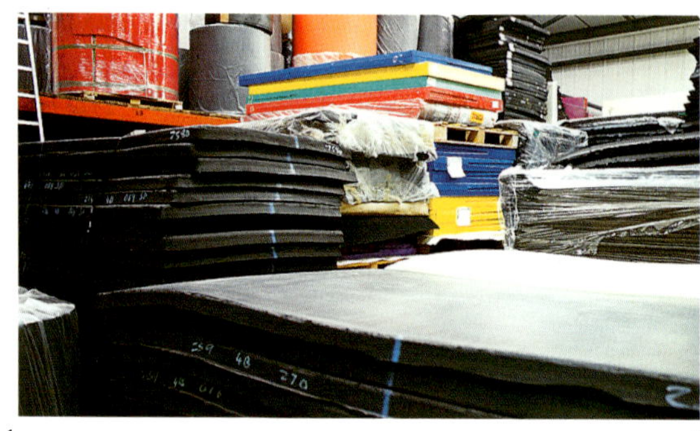

1 DETAIL FROM DRAWINGS OF
FIGURES WITH NOTES ON COLOUR

2 MATERIALS FOR THE SHOWER
CURTAIN IN THE FACTORY

3 EARLY DRAWING FOR THE
SHOWER CURTAIN

Taking a shower can be a private time. I wanted the figures in the shower curtain to reflect the relationships between people. Children may see the figures as innocently playing, whilst adults will perhaps see the relationships between the figures as a metaphor for human relationships.

My primary interest was in working with a plastic-based foam. Therefore it was important to find a company that had a knowledge of the materials and techniques and which would be willing to experiment and consider new tooling procedures. The company we found had not made a shower curtain before, but was willing and interested to work on this project to design a new product.

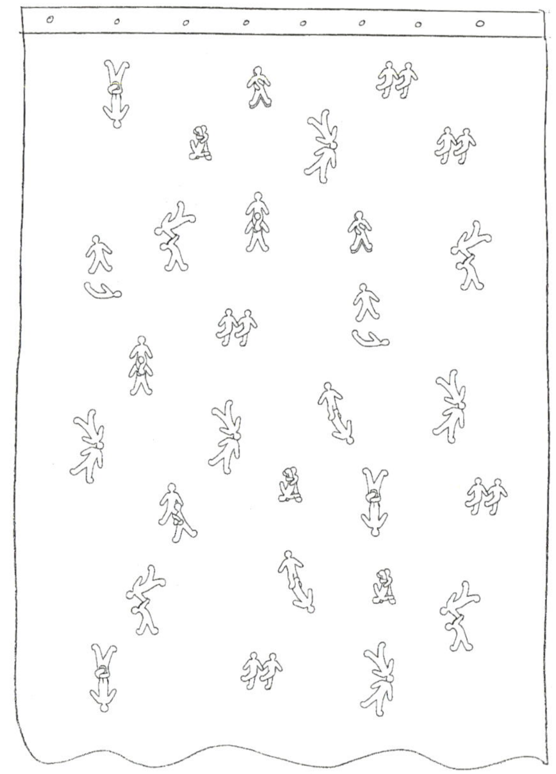

3

THE FINAL SHOWER CURTAIN

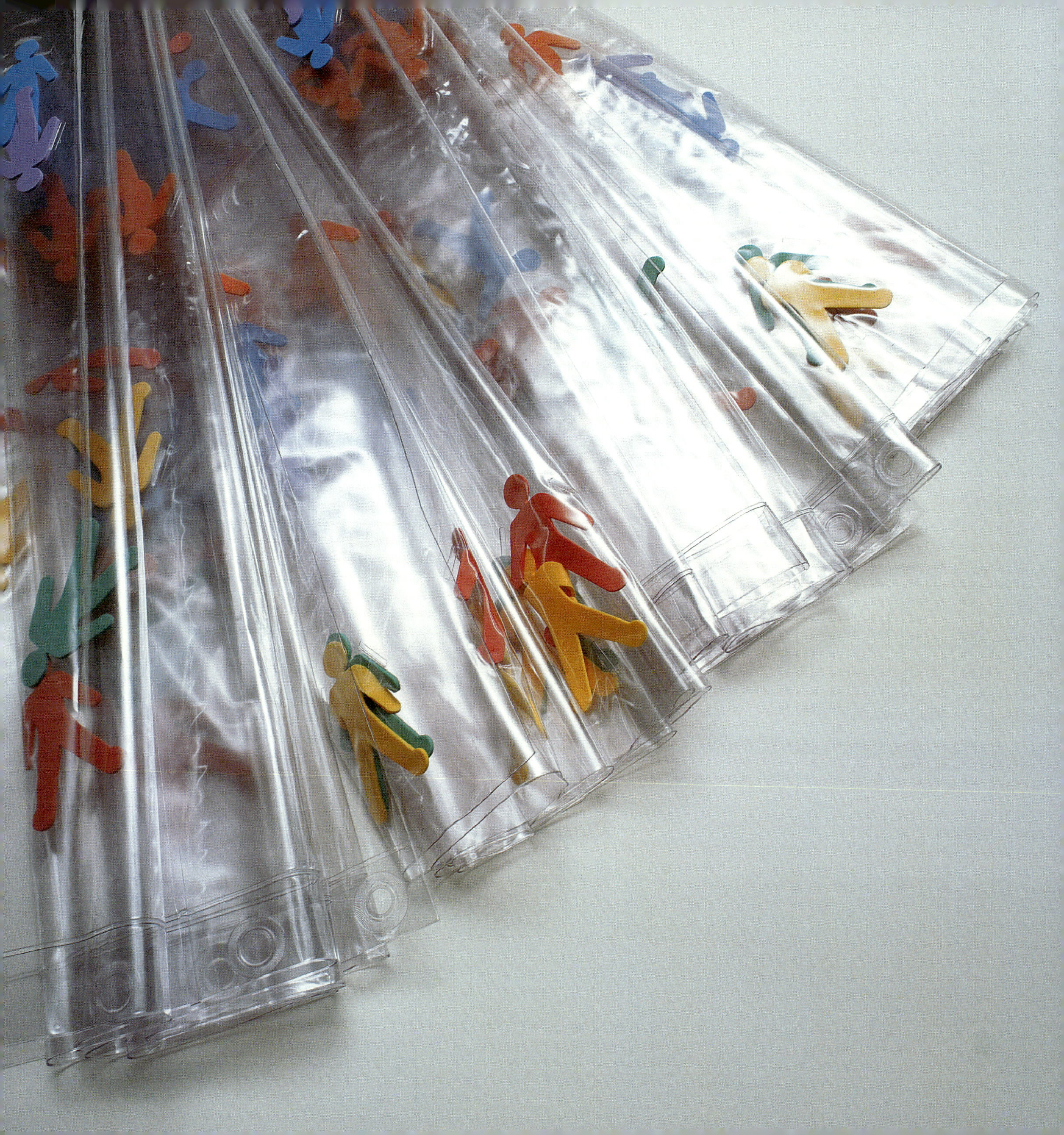

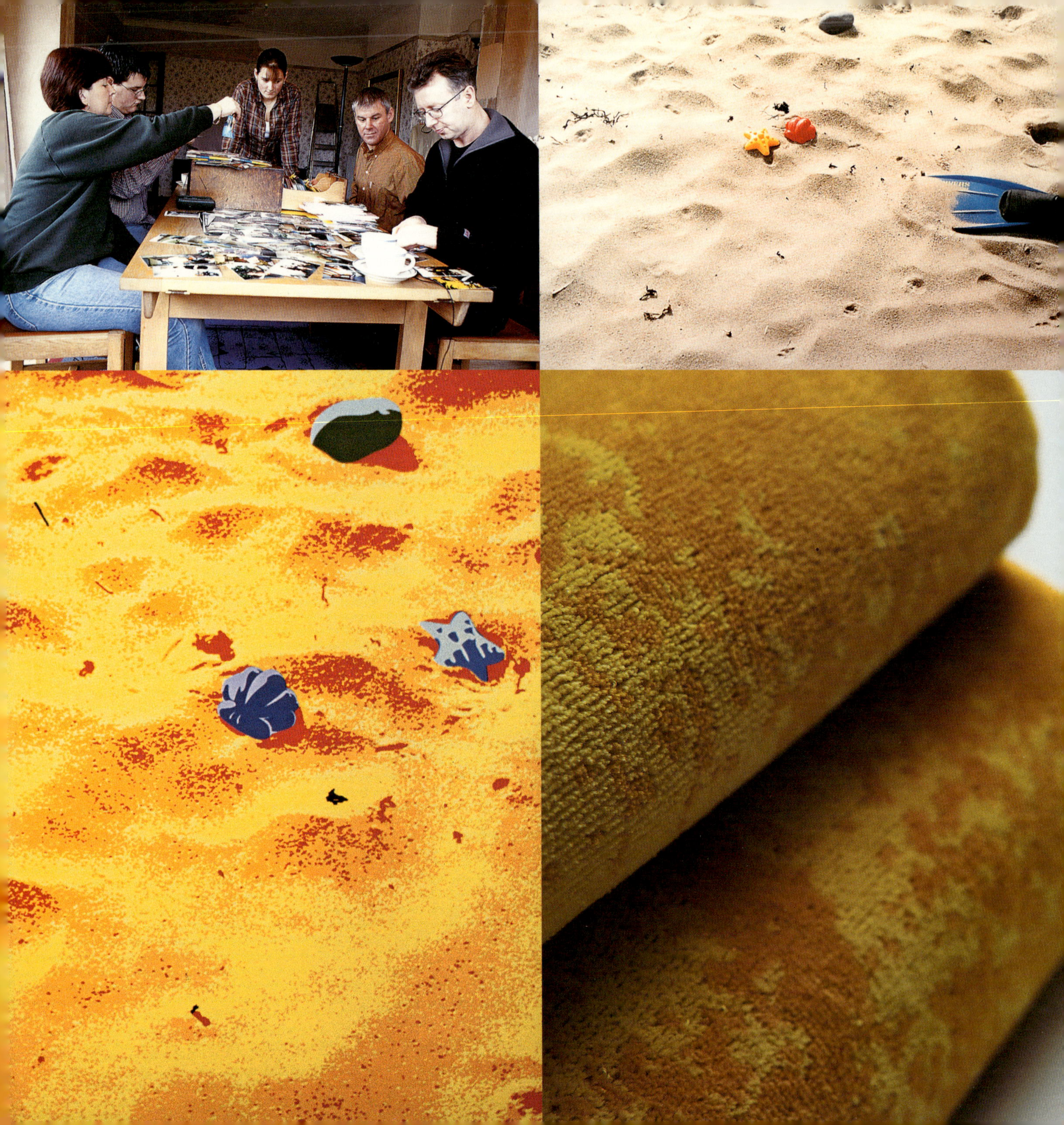

David Mach

ZADOCK, 1997
WIRE COATHANGERS
PRIVATE COLLECTION, TEL AVIV

Colin Painter: David Mach's long-standing commitment to reaching wide audiences meant that he was particuarly well-disposed to this project. After an encouraging start David Mach's progress through the project proved frustratingly slow – through no fault of his own. He left the Whittingtons full of ideas related to the way that family holidays figured in their lives. He played with the possibility of incorporating the family on holiday in an image or series of images. The idea of putting a piece of beach on a travel or picnic rug closely followed and Mach visited a carpet warehouse in central London which import rugs from India. There he identified the kind of fabric he wanted and supplied a simplified photograph of a section of beach to be woven into it.

The image was sent to two factories in India and samples were eagerly awaited. They took much longer than expected. When the rugs did arrive, they were not what Mach had hoped for. Given the time it had taken to produce the first samples there was no time to attempt improvements with the same manufacturers. Faster communications were established with José Machado de Almeida, a manufacturer in Portugal, and Mach dashed there late in the day. Impressed by the plant and the quality of the work he agreed a way forward with a modified image suited to their facilities. The transformation of the idea into a beach towel was a part of that process.

The Scottish beach photographed for the towel had a personal significance for the artist which connected with his own sense of 'home'. The wit and scale of most of Mach's work may obscure such dimensions. The beach towel combines these elements with characteristic humour, inventiveness and pragmatism in the face of the constraints imposed by mass production.

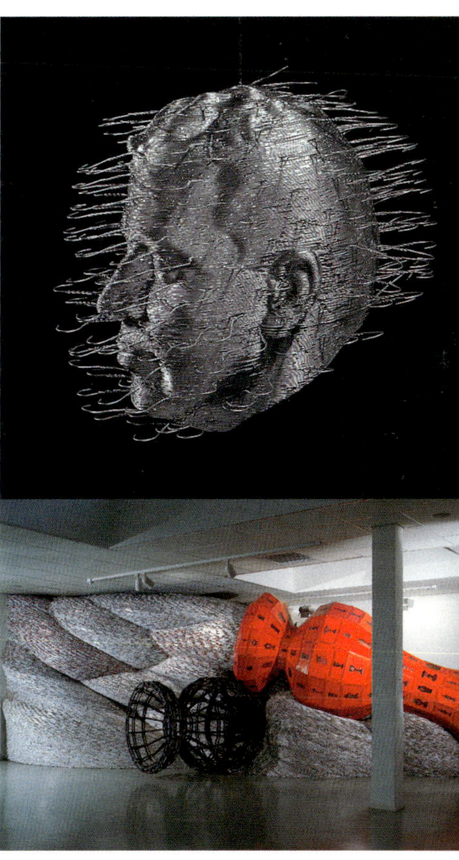

FRAMED, 1996
MAGAZINES AND HARALD VLUGT SCULPTURE
INSTALLATION: GALERIE DE LA TOUR, AMSTERDAM

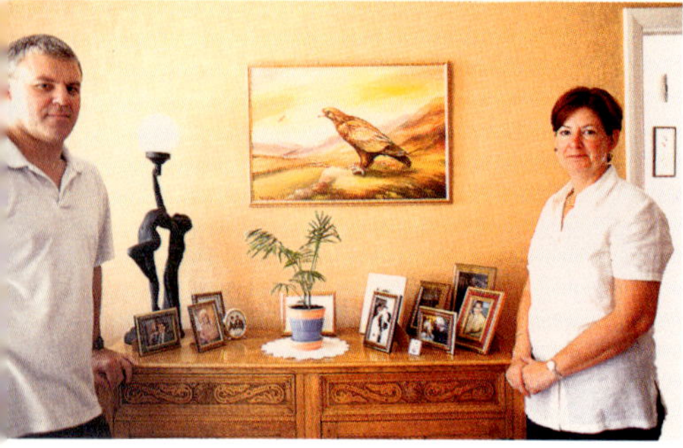

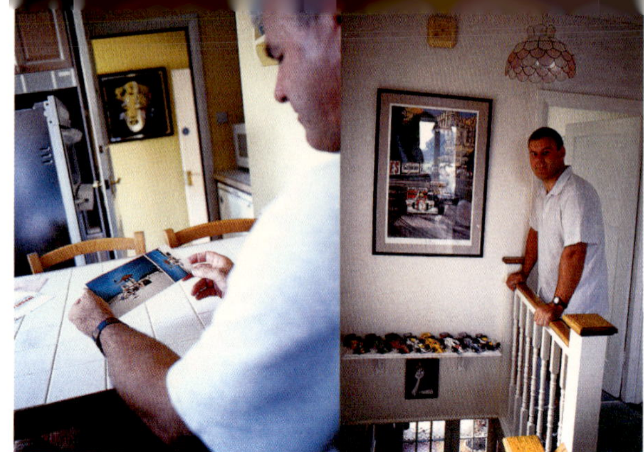

1 2 3

Clive and **Jan Whittington** (teenage son and daughter)

JAN: We collaborate in making most decisions about what we have in the house. We don't have many disagreements. Once Clive bought some wallpaper for the bedroom and we got two sheets up and I said, 'This is awful' and we took it down.

CLIVE: Normally we go out together to buy things. We chose the two oil paintings together. We got them from a friend who paints for pleasure. We admire the skill in his paintings. It's important that they are originals. If they were prints or photographs they wouldn't have the same impact.

JAN: Our family holidays are very important to us. We take a lot of photographs – so many that we file them to keep them under control. We've had summer holidays in Portugal, twice in Florida, and this year we're going to Malta. Occasionally we bring back souvenirs. When we went to Portugal we were decorating the kitchen so we bought a plate.

CLIVE: The motor-racing things are mine – the collection of models of Formula One cars and the signed limited-edition print of Nigel Mansell and Ayrton Senna. That's quite spooky really because I bought that print the day before Senna died. It was not like me to decide I had to have something like that.

JAN: Some things we've received as gifts I keep on display out of loyalty. People have taken the trouble to give them and I think they should be kept out on display.

CLIVE: In Woking there's a shop called Formula One World and you can buy a slick tyre with a glass top on it that's a coffee table. I'd like something like that. I saw an advert the other day, you know the flying ducks that people used to have? Well, they do pewter Formula One cars …

JAN: I don't want flying cars on the wall! I'm sorry. Clive won't let me have a picture of Cliff Richard on the wall but I've got to have racing cars and Marilyn Monroe.

CLIVE: We've got a small bronze Venus de Milo in the lounge and a larger cement version in the garden. I think of our pictures as art but not the three-dimensional things. That goes back to school days. In art lessons you did painting.

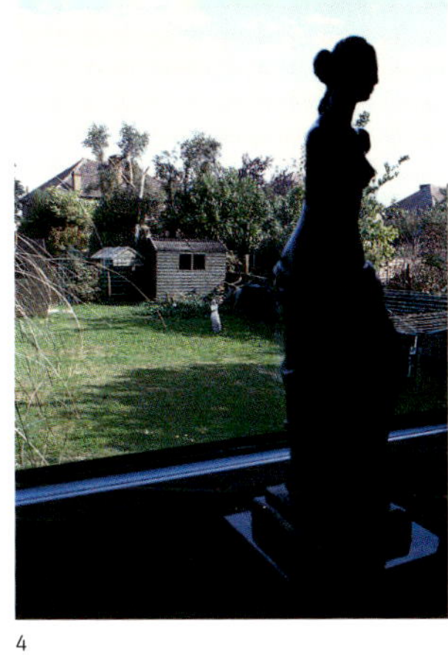

4

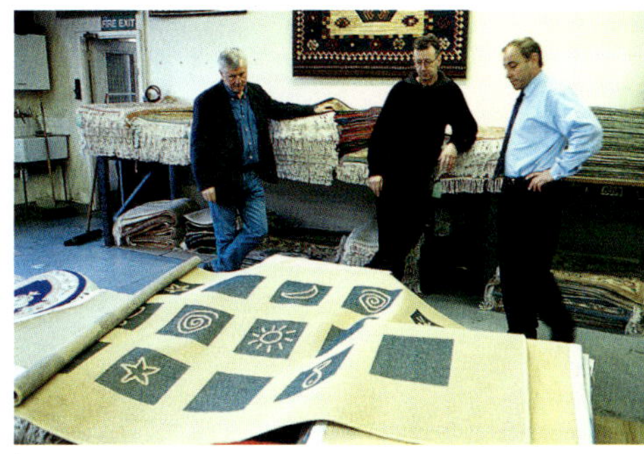

5

1 CLIVE AND JAN WHITTINGTON IN THEIR HOME

2 CLIVE WITH BEACH HOLIDAY SNAP

3 CLIVE WITH HIS CAR-RACING MEMORABILIA

4 THE WHITTINGTON FAMILY'S VENUS DE MILOS

5 DAVID MACH LOOKING AT RUG SAMPLES

David Mach

Making a beach towel is a new thing for me. I usually make one thing out of many things and here we are making one thing that will become many things through mass production. That's good for me, it gets me off that track.

I do have quite a lot of ideas for design but they're quite difficult to deal with. I could make ten works of art in the time it takes one design to evolve into a commercial product. I don't think an artist should be someone who works in a straight line making things of a similar flavour or style all the time, but I do think an artist should be producing many ideas to be realized in a variety of ways. I like the idea of the artist as 'idea-monger'.

If you're going to make a work of art that is going to reach somebody – lots of somebodies – then you have to start with people. People are the most important part of a project like this. It was very valuable visiting the Whittingtons and talking to them. Looking at the photographs of their family holidays obviously had a big influence on me. In fact the idea for a beach towel grew from those meetings.

The beach I photographed for the image on the towel is close to where I grew up in Fife – one of the most beautiful beaches in the country. I spent many hours on that beach as a boy, so the image is not haphazardly chosen, it's very personal. Perhaps it relates to notions of home, roots.

Originally I tried to keep a couple of objects on the towel – a shell and a star – but the manufacturing process meant using only a couple of colours. In fact I ended up simplifying the image considerably,

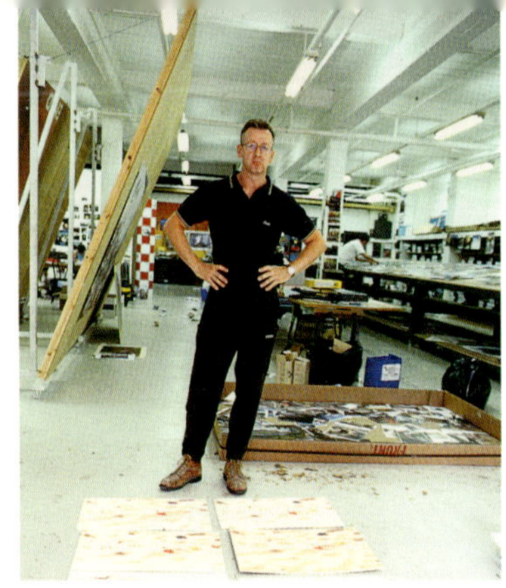

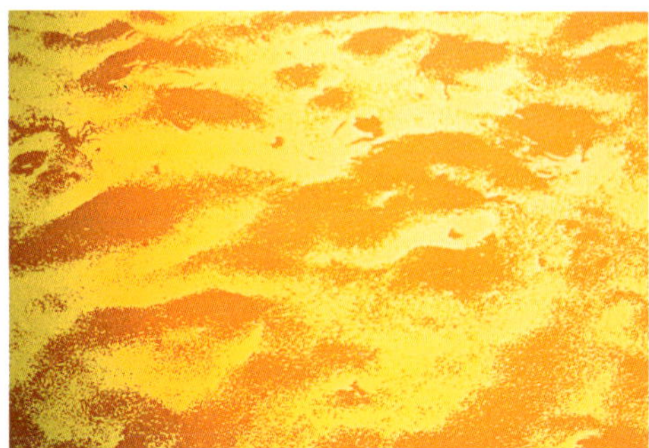

right down to two colours. I still like it, I still think it's the same idea although it amuses me to think I was only one colour away from producing a self-coloured towel.

I think the idea includes people, a picture of a little bit of beach that is your own. You might not just buy a towel for yourself but for someone else as a gift. Having the beach towel on sale in Homebase means that a wide range of people can come across it and buy it to use for their own purposes.

I think Homebase is a great place to show art but of course you've got to do it right, you can't think of it as a gallery. It's not that pure.

THE FINAL BEACH TOWEL

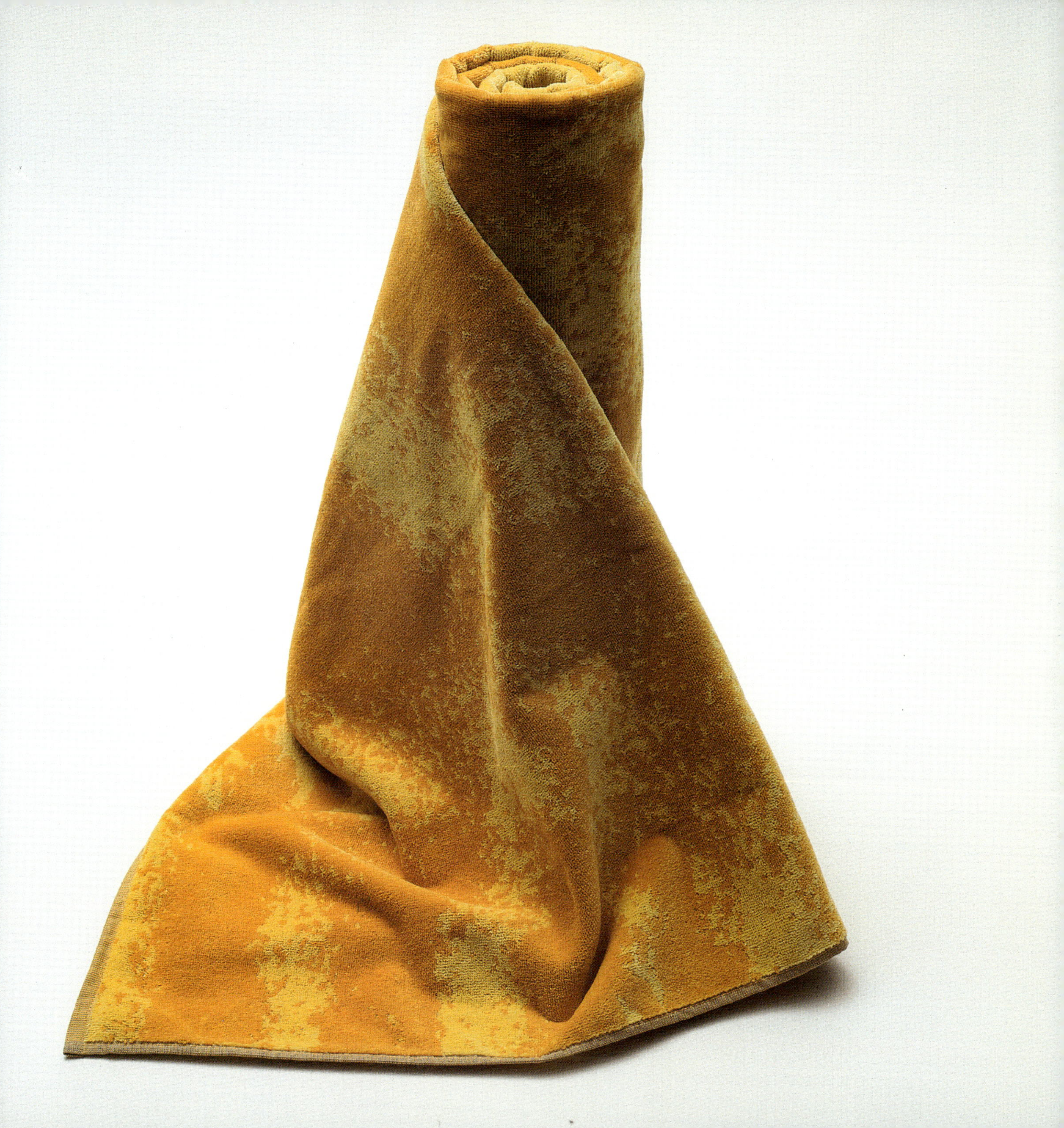

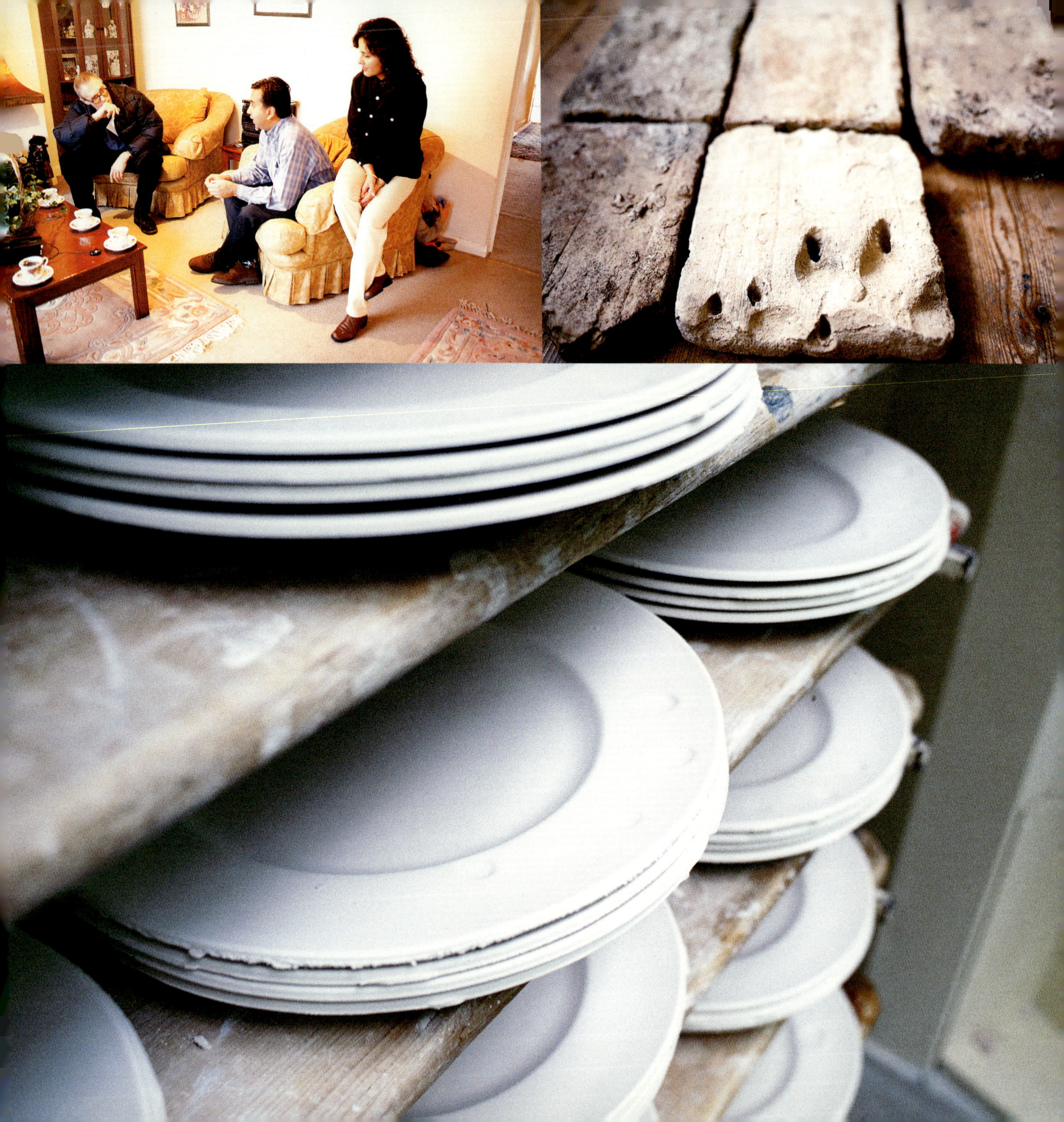

Richard Wentworth

Colin Painter: Whatever other reasons Richard Wentworth had for choosing to work in clay, one was that the material (not to mention the resulting humble plate) spoke with an elemental dignity resonant of the Mandalia home.

The decision to use clay led easily to Royal Doulton. There the artist quickly struck up a strong working relationship with Peter Allen, Director of Shape, Design and Development. It was a relationship built on mutual respect and a shared concern to 'do it properly' as Wentworth puts it. Touring the Royal Doulton plant Wentworth was impressed by the number of people that handled each piece of pottery on its journey from raw clay to finished product – indispensable people with consummate skills in playing their particular parts yet without trace of elevated perception of themselves or their abilities. He also noticed that the production of industrial ceramics strove to eliminate evidence of human touch – marks which would be considered blemishes. It was his sense of this as a signifi-cant paradox that provided the foundation for the plate that he ultimately produced. That is not to undervalue other dimensions in the piece, in particular its reference to traditions of ceramic decoration. Richard Wentworth has for years brought a distinctive intelligence to the observation of everyday objects and their construction. This plate is no exception.

His ambition to decorate a plate with his fingerprints in relief demanded ingenuity from Royal Doulton. In Peter Allen's words: 'It required Richard to be part of the model-making process from which the production moulds would be made. Normally, a plate is made from plastic clay face down on a plaster mould which, by the time it is handleable, is leather hard and will not take fingerprint impressions. So that Richard could form an imprint into soft clay, special moulds were made and the plates formed, in effect, in reverse. As the mould was removed from the machine he was able to experiment with prints before deciding which impression would then go forward to form the master mould.'

FALSE CEILING, 1995 (PARTIAL VIEW)
BOOKS AND STEEL CABLE
COURTESY LISSON GALLERY

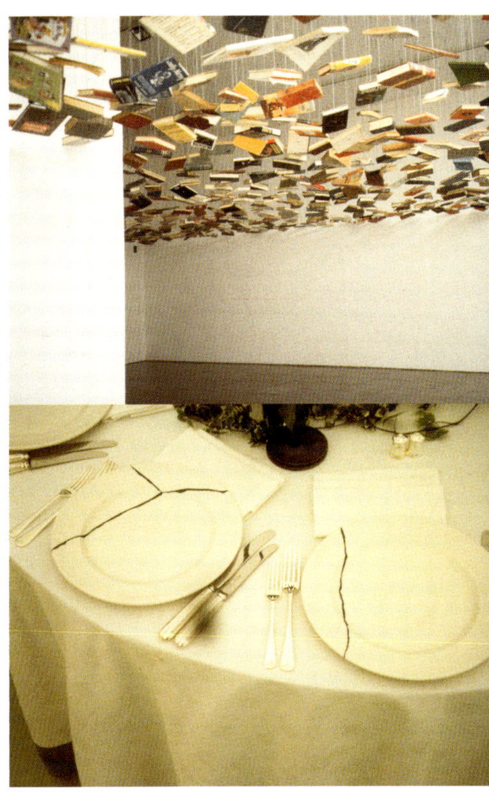

SERPENTINE GALLERY GALA DINNER IN THE PRESENCE
OF DIANA, PRINCESS OF WALES, 28 JUNE 1995
REPAIRED PLATES, EDITION OF 450, CERAMIC AND EPOXY
MULTIPLE OWNERS

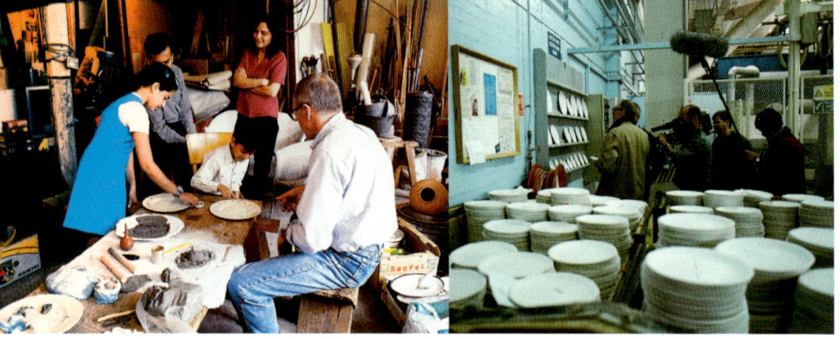

Sunil and **Varsha Mandalia** (son aged seven and daughter aged eleven)

SUNIL: We are a Hindu family and quite religious. For us the most important images in our home are of the
saint called Jalaram Bapa. He is one of the saints that our family has a great pull towards. He is the
family choice of saint. My dad and my grandma live with us. When we pray we think of Jalaram Bapa
more-so than Lord Krishna or Lord Rama who is the ultimate god in our religion. Every morning grandma
makes offerings to the gods.

VARSHA: A picture of Jalaram Bapa is inside the front door so that when we go out we can think of him. It
also gives us a feeling of security and warmth like someone's watching over us.

SUNIL: We have a mixture of things around us and that just shows where we are. You can't totally separate
yourself from what you are and you can't separate yourself from where you are.

VARSHA: The things we have around us are pleasing to the eye and we try to keep a balance to please other
people as well. We want things that welcome people, that are down to earth and simple.

SUNIL: The picture in the corner is of Mahatma Gandhi. It used to be over there where the picture of my
mother is now. I'm a great admirer of Mahatma Gandhi but last year my mum passed away and I
replaced him with my favourite picture of her. Because of the way the room is arranged my mum's
picture is more prominent.

VARSHA: The glass cabinet has souvenirs and school photos through the years, photos of friends. The
coconut embroidered over is an object people carry on good occasions – at weddings for example, a
bridesmaid carries it on her head to welcome the groom. On the top of the cabinet is a sculpture of a
devotee of Lord Krishna called Meerabai.

SUNIL: We have a picture of Lord Krishna dancing. It's such a beautiful picture. Lord Krishna was very much
a lady's man. He had so many women after him and they all wanted to dance. In this picture he's
dancing with all of them at the same time. He's staying in the middle and he's made them believe that
he's dancing with all of them.

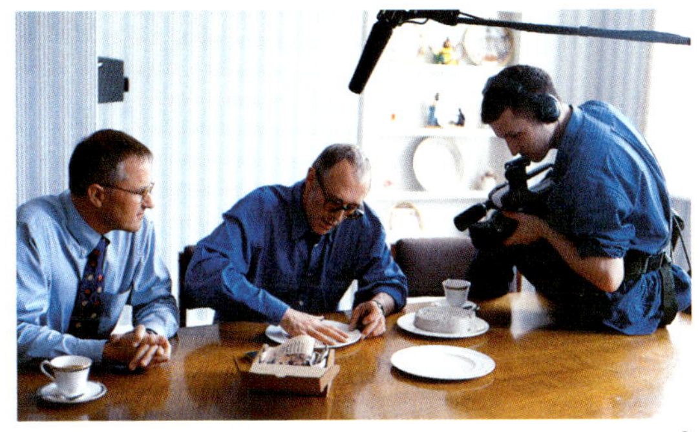

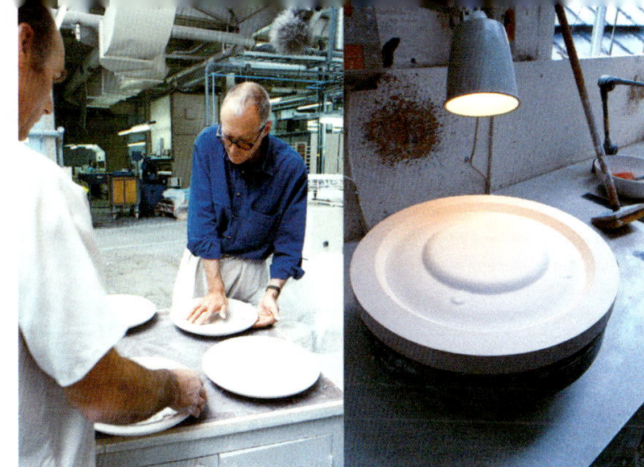

3

4

5

Richard Wentworth

I visited the household with apprehension but discovered, by doing it, a kind of human contract
was forged in mutual exchange. Once that contract was in play there was something quite extraordinary
happening that really couldn't happen any other way. Meeting the Mandalias had a powerful effect. They
are so dignified, so modest about their lives, beliefs and achievements. I felt enriched and humbled.

> The strangest thing about plates is that when you sit down to eat you get your own, but the
> moment you finish it's somebody else's. Plates operate in a complex world of manners, sharedness,
> separation – a public/private thing, enormously widely experienced. This makes them very special.

The idea of making something that might lead an ordinary life, perhaps get broken and thrown away, was
very attractive. I like vulnerability. It's probably a vanitas thing – we're all here but apparently not for very
long. To an archaeologist rubbish is probably more important than the brilliant sculpture, the effigy.
Rubbish can be more telling about human values, ambitions.

> Travelling on a train I might think, what enables it to be here? What makes it run? There is this vast
> pile of invisible skills – some managerial, people who understand timetables, and others who have
> to get their hands incredibly dirty. There would be no world without a lot of dirty handling. Many
> people who get their hands dirty don't know how appreciated they are. As with trains, so with plates.

It was a pleasure to work with an operation the size of Royal Doulton. That level of competence,
professional expectation – completely to do with ideas of 'quality'. I wanted to do something properly.

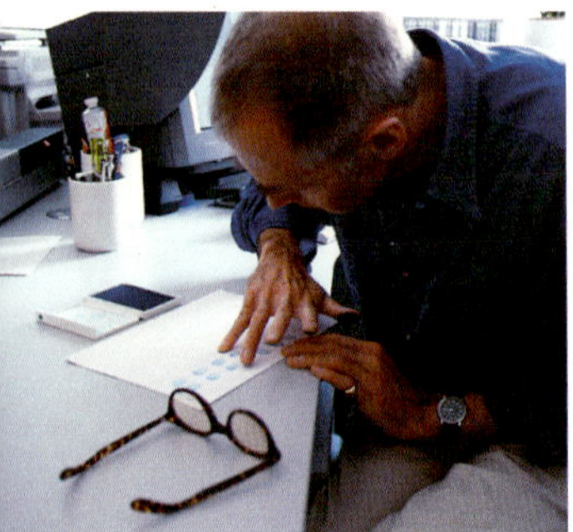
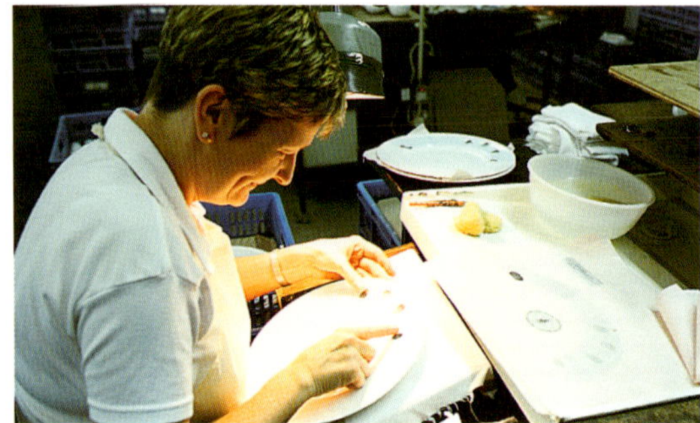
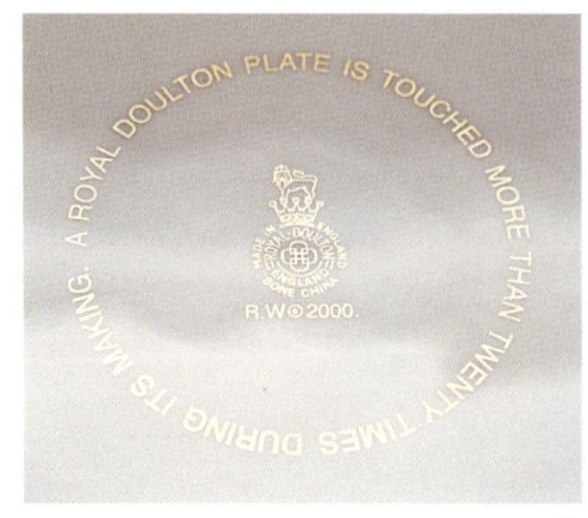

The eye of this project's needle is the market. We are all handed the market place as a fact of contemporary life. I was very aware of the narrow gap through which I had to pass. Can it be done? How much will it cost? It's made me think about all the stuff around me in the market place – all optimistically projected into space.

Art is always talked about as if it didn't take place within constraints. But art is dripping with constraints. I don't think good problem solving is good art – but pictures have to get out of the studio door.

What is it that I think at home that I don't think in the studio? What is it that I think in the studio that I don't think at home? And what do I think in the gap between which, for me, is the street? I don't believe I'm hugely changed as the doors open and shut. It's all a big cavorting, thoughting, thinking process. Nevertheless the piles of plates in my studio are not a washing up job.

We are drowning in objects. Part of me feels guilty that I've just put another one in the world. Also, it's a multiple birth. In fact I feel much like people who have multiple births must feel. They thought they were up for one which is how most artists proceed but, through a twist in this particular project, we will end up with thousands. Professional designers only think in that way – their whole project is to unload half a million of something.

Being an artist is no less lonely than it ever was. One is just as insecure, unsure, self-critical. Through energy, perhaps some quality – or luck – artists may become more visible. Not much response comes back to the artist from that visibility. One thing I like about this project is the prospect of new and wider responses.

1 RICHARD WENTWORTH MAKING FINGERPRINTS FOR THE GOLD LEAF TRANSFERS WHICH WILL DECORATE THE IMPRESSIONS ON THE PLATE RIM, ROYAL DOULTON

2 ADDING GOLD LEAF FINGER-PRINTS, ROYAL DOULTON

3 THE BACK OF THE PLATE

THE FINAL PLATE

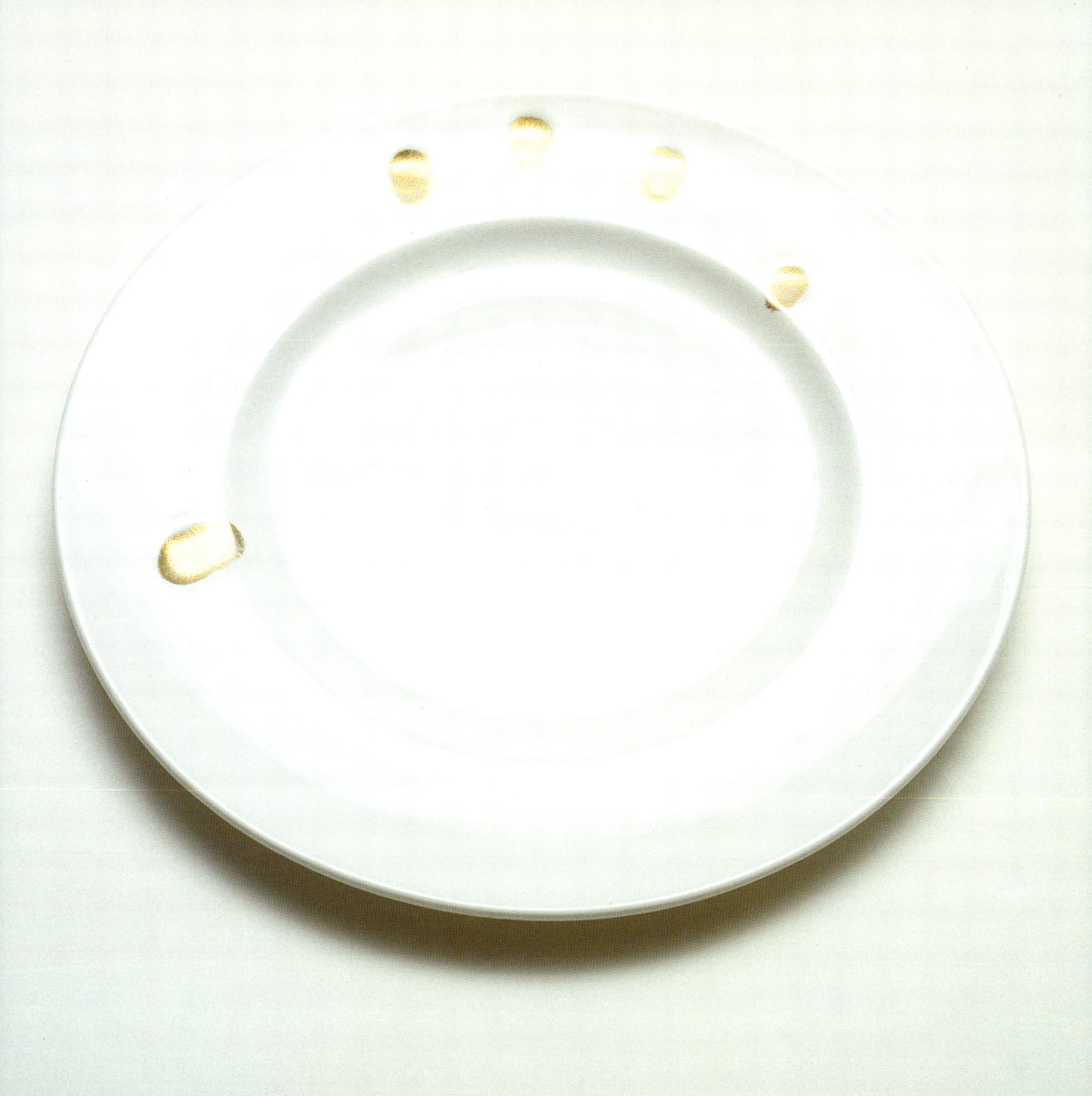

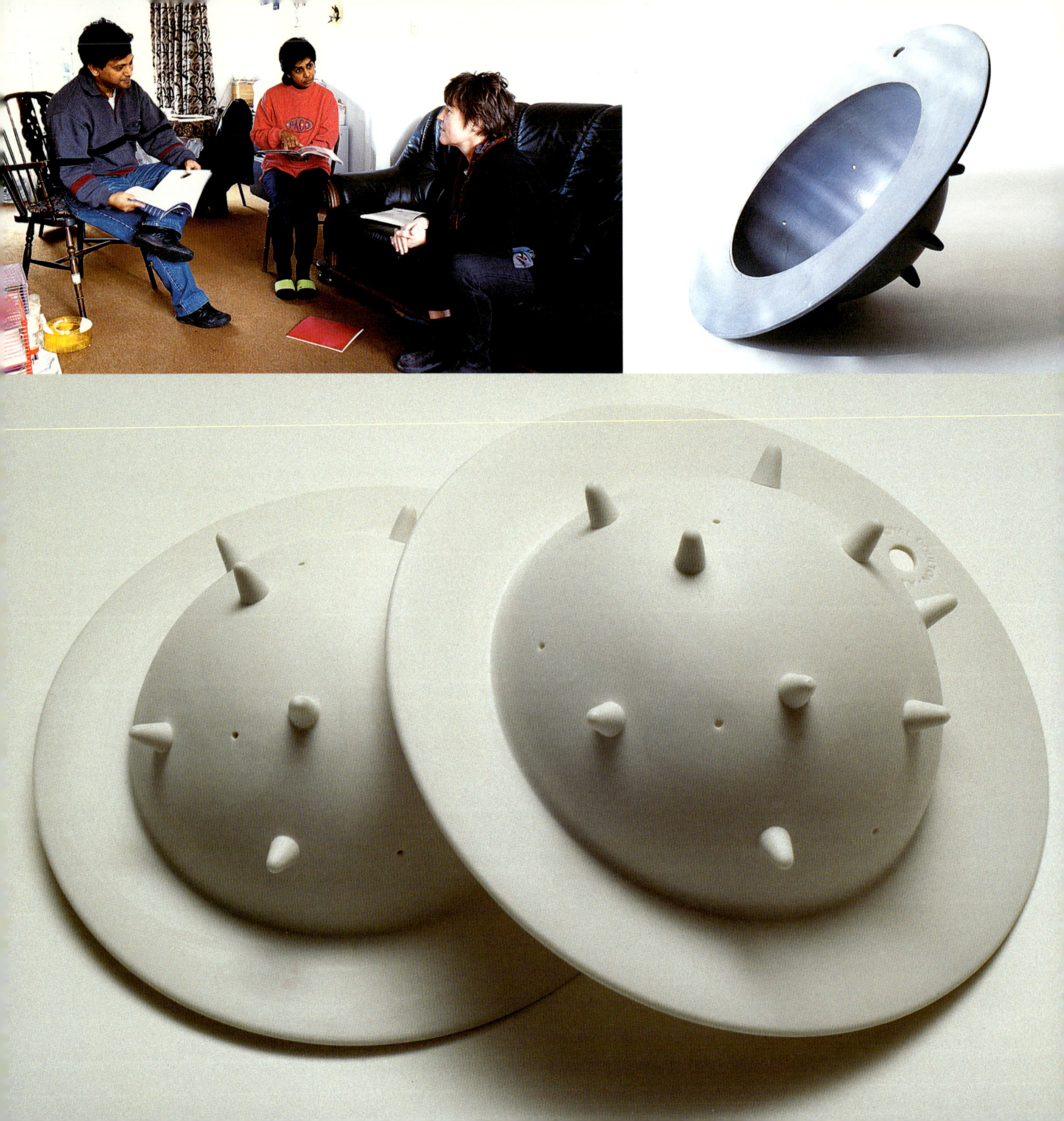

Alison Wilding

Colin Painter: Alison Wilding was the only artist in the project who, after an initial period of reflection, made the single prototype – already the size and form of the final object. From that moment the way forward consisted of the lengthy process of identifying appropriate materials in which to have it manufactured and a manufacturer able to do the job.

Aluminium was considered first but the little 'legs' on the sculpture made withdrawal from a mould impossible. Unacceptable modifications to the prototype would be necessary. Other solutions in aluminium were too expensive. Forms of plastic were explored but none of them were to Wilding's liking. Acrylic was under consideration when, on a visit to Royal Doulton, ceramic emerged as the ideal solution. In fine china, and with the technical resource and experience of Royal Doulton, it was possible to realize the sculpture without any need for modification to the prototype. In fact a small adjustment to the positioning of one of the legs was made, not for technical reasons, but as an improvement to the sculpture suggested by the artist.

While there are those who cannot resist describing it as a bowl (and it functions well as such) the sculpture defies the attribution of a single identity or orientation. Its ambiguity is characteristic of much of Wilding's earlier work but, as she explains later here, it also stems directly from her visit to the Sivalinghams.

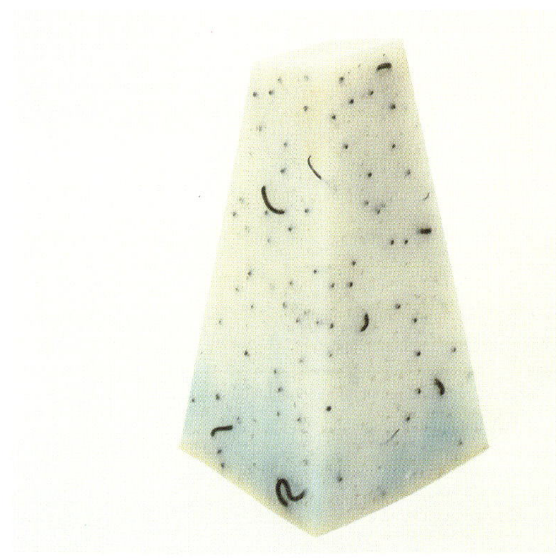

WIRED, 1997
SILICONE RUBBER, ELECTRICAL CABLE
COURTESY ROBERT MILLER GALLERY, NEW YORK
AND KARSTEN SCHUBERT, LONDON

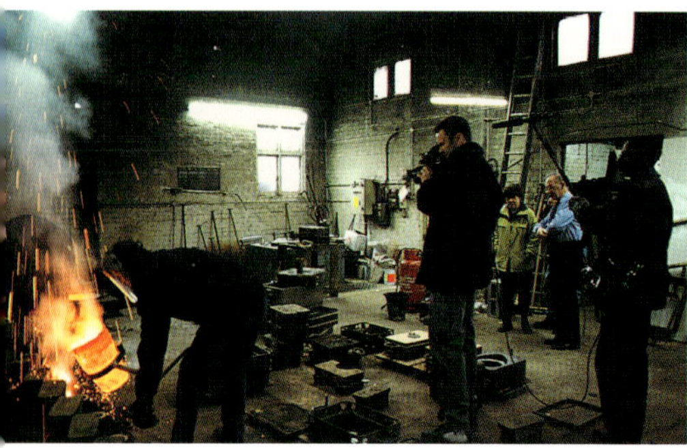

1

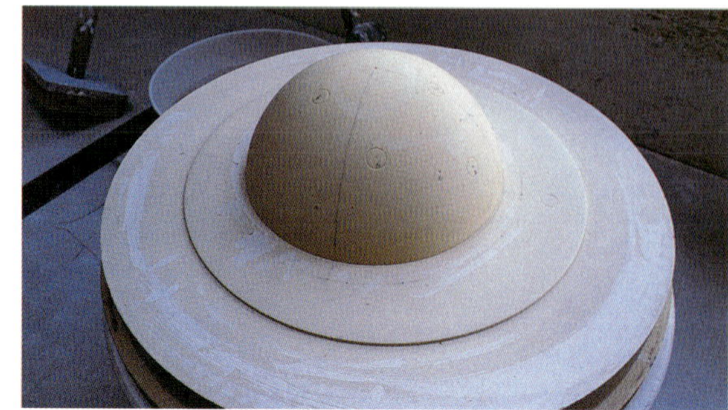

2

Siva and **Lalitha Sivalingham**   (two sons aged eleven and fourteen)

SIVA: This is a Hindu household. Both Lalitha and I are Tamils. I was born in Ceylon before it became Sri
Lanka and was brought up in a purely Tamil atmosphere. Lalita was born in Singapore in a more multi-
cultural environment. Our home reflects these different backgrounds – a mixture of cultural influences.

LALITHA: When we came to this house we had mostly Chinese things around us . . . It was so Chinese that
when people visited us from Singapore they would say, 'We wanted it to look English!' But I thought
about it and decided it would confuse my boys if I made it too English.

SIVA: Our friends and relatives in England also have a mixture of English and Indian things. As children grow
up here they bring their own art and tastes into the home. We bring our boys up to be open – but they
come with us to the temple and when we go to traditional weddings they wear their costumes.

LALITHA: We still have a Chinese good luck sign. It means a lot to us because when Cumaren was born he
was very premature and we didn't know whether he was going to make it. One of my friends visited and
gave the sign to me. Everything turned out well so we have never taken it down.

SIVA: We had two glass cases full of things – gifts and souvenirs – but we got rid of one. The remaining case
has the more meaningful things that we kept. I remember we had a glass cabinet in my home in Ceylon.
We also displayed pictures, posters and portraits of my grandfather and father.

LALITHA: One thing that people tend to display in Hindu homes is a portrait of their god and goddess. Our
main god is the elephant Ganesh. Every Friday I cook something special for Ganesh and offer it.

SIVA: I like to paint but I rarely get the time these days. Drawing is quite useful to me in my work as an
engineer. But I would like to find time to paint landscapes.

LALITHA: In Singapore we had a neighbour who used to give us a calendar with pictures of British
countryside on it. So beautiful. We learned a poem at school about golden daffodils. I remember a
poem about autumn leaves and had no idea what it meant. In fact a lot of things we learned at school
only became meaningful when I came here.

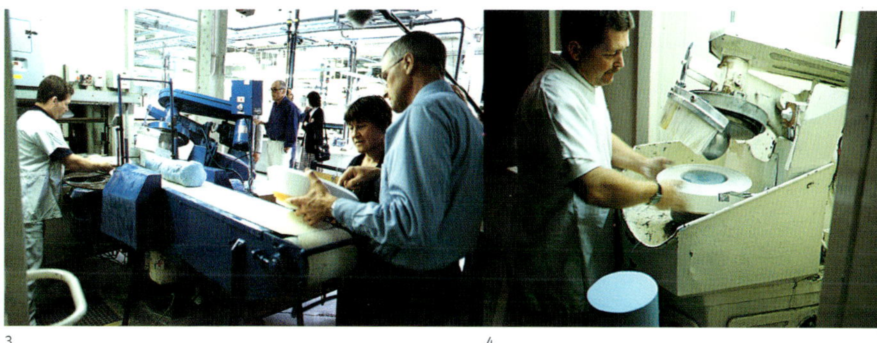

Alison Wilding

I was intrigued with the idea of mass production which goes much further than a limited edition and reaches more people. I'd never thought about art objects doing that. I'm interested in reaching a wider public without compromising on what I do. It's people's access to art that is the problem, not their capacity to deal with it.

> Immediately after visiting the Sivalinghams I hadn't a clue what I was going to do. I got very near to despair with production deadlines approaching. Actually, I think I intellectualized it too much – analysing my visit to the family and how I could make sense of it. When I stopped trying to make sense of it and began working with materials – with the knowledge of having been to the home – things began to work out.

One thing I took from my visit, which affected me a lot, was that it was a household which appeared to reconcile very disparate engagements. Siva works for British Aerospace investigating new materials – on the forefront of knowledge about how things are made – at the same time the family offers libations to the household gods. I found that juxtaposition extraordinary. So I thought about an object that might be a hybrid – a fusion that might appeal to both aspects of the household. What has resulted is certainly a fusion in the sense that it might or might not be functional.

> I don't know if this piece is functional or not – there is no definitive way of placing it. Its transformation from prototype to fine china has given it a translucency so it has also become an object that holds light.

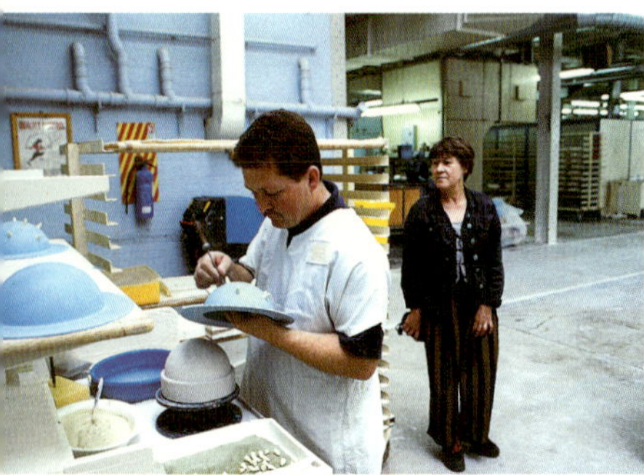

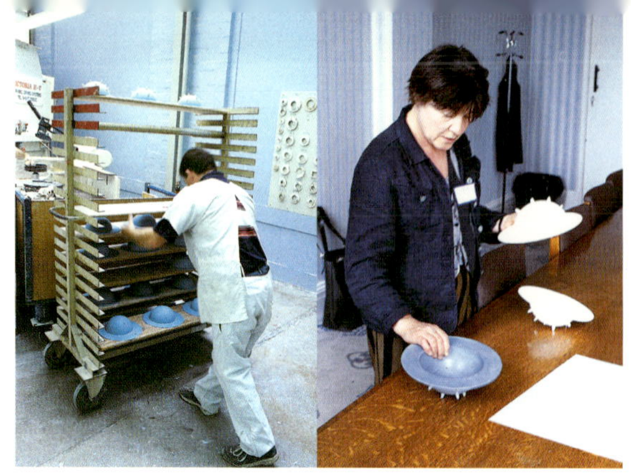

1 ADDING THE 'LEGS' BY HAND, ROYAL DOULTON

2 SCULPTURES READY FOR THE KILN, ROYAL DOULTON

3 ALISON WILDING WITH FINISHED SCULPTURES AND HER ORIGINAL PROTOTYPE

It was interesting that I made a form – a prototype – without being sure what materials it would ultimately be mass-produced in. But when I think of all the things it might have been made of I'm sure that fine china was best suited to it. If I were a designer I probably would have done it differently – but I'm not.

I don't think I've ever made something which can be used and displayed in so many different ways. Usually my work has a definite orientation. The nature of the project has brought this about.

I like to think that my work rewards attention over time and has several layers to penetrate. This possibility is particularly strong in the home where people can live with the work.

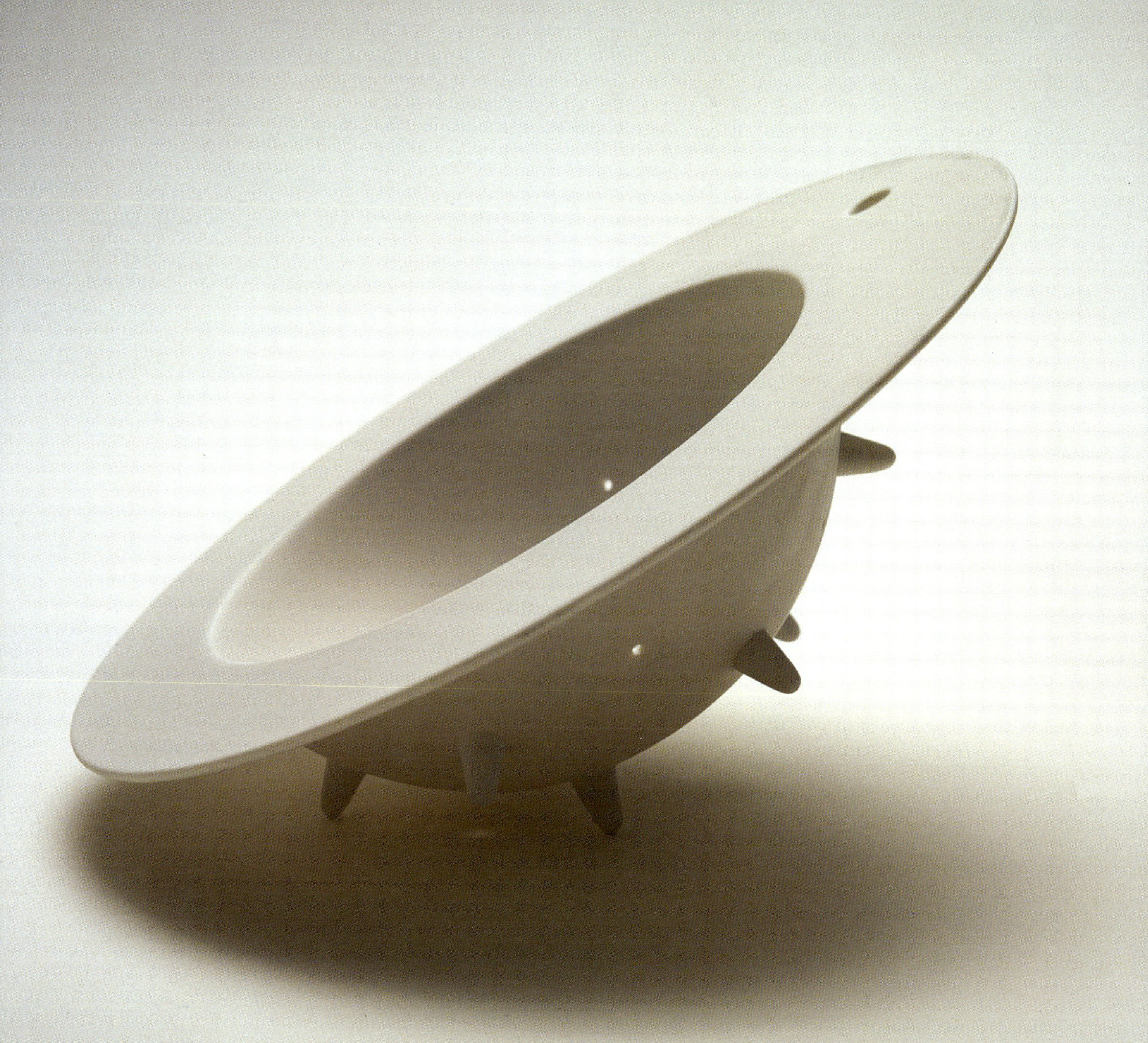